Crosscurrents / MODERN CRITIQUES

Harry T. Moore, *General Editor*

Twentieth-Century Russian Literature

Harry T. Moore and Albert Parry

WITH A PREFACE BY

Harry T. Moore

SOUTHERN ILLINOIS UNIVERSITY PRESS
Carbondale and Edwardsville

FEFFER & SIMONS, INC.
London and Amsterdam

Library of Congress Cataloging in Publication Data

Moore, Harry Thornton.
  Twentieth-century Russian literature.

  (Crosscurrents/modern critiques)
  Bibliography: p.
  1. Russian literature—20th century—History and
criticism. I. Parry, Albert, 1901–   joint author.
II. Title.
PG3017.M6   891.7'09   74–13812
ISBN 0–8093–0703–0

Contents

Foreword

No literature in the modern world has artistic, philosophical, or psychological ingredients or values alone. Inevitably it is also a sociopolitical expression, whether or not the prose writers and the poets in question consciously set out to articulate such thoughts and emotions.

For specific historical Russian reasons, this is particularly valid for Russian literature of all recent and current eras. As this was true of the great Golden Age of Russian literature in the nineteenth century, so it was in the Silver Age of the twentieth century up to the Revolution of 1917, and even more so in the Soviet period since the Communist takeover of the nation in that momentous year. At all times Russian literature is a mirror of its people's grievances, protests, and aspirations. What the tsars and the commissars have prohibited or curtailed on the political arena, what the police and the censors have denied to the people in its civil liberties, the people's bold and rare talents—its writers and other artists—have sought to voice, sometimes at great risks to their own personal freedom and even lives, through novels and short stories, through poems and stage plays and, latterly, through films.

But the effect often has also been the cause. The mirror has spoken up in magic and disturbing tones as a call to dissent and action. Itself a child of sociopolitical dreams and demands, Russian literature has ever been a mighty instrument and influence upon the societal fabric and the body politic of that gifted nation. In the nineteenth century

Alexander Pushkin's daring poems and Ivan Turgenev's moving stories made their contribution toward the freeing of the serfs in 1861. And the Revolutions of 1905 and 1917 were at least predicted if not hastened by Fyodor Dostoyevsky's clairvoyant novels and Anton Chekhov's melancholy dramas. In our own 1960s and '70s the *samizdat* or underground-press editions of the trenchant works by Boris Pasternak and Alexander Solzhenitsyn are not alone the artistic and faithful reflections of the people's dissatisfactions but also the tocsin calling men and women to civic awareness and warning their leaders and masters to mend their violent and unjust ways.

Today, as in the past, the good Russian writer is not only a marvelous stylist; not alone a sensitive portrayer of his country's landscapes lit by its sunsets; not just a psychologist or a philosopher ably scalpelling his fellows' hearts and souls, his men's and women's loves and hates. He is a fearless citizen above all else. As Solzhenitsyn put it in his Nobel Prize acceptance speech of 1970 (undelivered because of the Soviet government's ban but, luckily, publicized widely in 1972 nonetheless): "Russian literature has long been familiar with the notions that a writer can do much within his society and that it is his duty to do so."

But is it the concern of the Russian writer and no other? Indeed not, Solzhenitsyn proclaims: The whole world "is being inundated by the brazen conviction that power can do anything, justice nothing." So it behooves writers and artists in the entire world, and not in the Soviet Union alone, to give their best and utmost to the noble task of resisting violence and lies: "Writers and artists can conquer falsehood. In the struggle with falsehood, art always did win and it always does win! One word of truth shall outweigh the whole world."

ALBERT PARRY

Greenwich, Connecticut
June 1974

Preface

In the Foreword, Albert Parry has touched upon the most important elements for a consideration of twentieth-century Russian literature, particularly the close relationship between the life and the literature of that country, not only in the case of the great authors of that country's past, but also in that of the present. Its writers, whether they produce tragedy, comedy, or other kinds of literature, are not superficial. Indeed, most of the characters in Russian imaginative writing are what E. M. Forster in his famous book on the novel defined as "round" ("capable of surprising in a convincing way") rather than what he called "flat" ("constructed round a single idea or quality"); the former are more important in novels, but Forster sees advantages in having at least some of the flat characters to fill out the work and give it balance; and, much as he admires the great Russian writers, he rather ruefully notes that their novels seldom contain flat characters, though "they would be a decided help." Somehow, in that enormous Russian landscape, the tendency of the inhabitants is, in terms of character, toward the round. The people are intensely concerned with every aspect of existence, and their writers, dealing with all the depths of experience, recognize the importance of the sociopolitical in modern life, as Dr. Parry has pointed out, in the present book and elsewhere: it is one of the elements that keeps Russian literature so exciting, from the days when Dostoyevsky and Tolstoy turned out such novels as The Possessed and War and Peace, which among so much else have an enormous amount of sociopolitical content.

The form of the present volume somewhat resembles that of my books on Twentieth-Century French Literature and Twentieth-Century German Literature, but in this later book I have had the honor of working with Dr. Albert Parry, a good friend for almost forty years who recently retired from Colgate University, where he had for many years been chairman of the Department of Russian Studies. He is an expert of highest standing on Russian affairs, and frequently discusses them in the leading journals and on national television programs, and he has written numerous books on the subject as well as his contributions to our fuller understanding of American life in such books as Garrets and Pretenders: A History of Bohemianism in America and Whistler's Father.

Dr. Parry and I sometimes differ a bit on literary judgments, but in our collaboration here he has usually allowed me to express my own determinations of value—a statement which is necessary because I'd consider it unfair if he were to be held responsible for certain opinions which are definitely my own. The reader will not always find it possible to discover exactly which parts of the book are mine and which are Albert Parry's since we worked together rather closely in every phase of the book; in the main, however, most of the earlier chapters are predominantly mine, with numerous corrections and additions (many of both merely suggestions by Professor Parry), while the later chapters are largely his own, appropriately so because he is so thoroughly acquainted with what goes on in today's Russia. Once again I must say that his willingness to work with me on this book makes me feel deeply honored. It is safe to say, I think, that no other volume we know of covers twentieth-century Russian literature so thoroughly, from Chekhov and his contemporaries to Solzhenitsyn and his; and I may add that the book because of Dr. Parry's expertness gives its reader a special view of Soviet Union communications, aboveground and underground.

Now a few matters of style must be mentioned; in the present volume these follow Professor Parry's determination of the best way to present Russian names and terms in English. We don't, for example, follow the system, now pretty well outmoded, of indicating the syllables to be accented in proper names. This was the method used, for example, in Peter Kropotkin's Ideals and Realities in Russian Literature (1905), in which we find Gógol, Tolstóy, and so on. The present book, on the other hand, includes what is called the "soft sign" after such letters as t, l, n, and others. But although the text will contain the mark after such names as Mashen'ka and Van'ka, it will omit this soft sign in the case of names well known in English-speaking countries, such as Pilnyak and Babel. We anglicize Joseph Stalin, but only approximately do this with Iosif Brodsky.

The names of old literary schools, such as the Symbolists and the Acmeists, have initial capitals, as do those of such groups, or their members, as Communism and Communists, Socialism, Socialists.

In my own case I should like to mention indebtedness to all the commentators on modern Russian literature whom I have read in English, but regrettably there is no space for that, since the full text of our book overruns the limitations for volumes in this series. I must, however, mention two recent books by Dr. Parry which are extremely valuable for anyone wishing to learn more about various phases of life in the Soviet Union beyond those of literature and its associated forms of communication: The New Class Divided and The Russian Scientist.

I am grateful to my wife Beatrice for her continued encouragement and to our good friend Carolyn Moe for her help in putting the manuscript into its final form.

HARRY T. MOORE

Southern Illinois University
August 2, 1974

Twentieth-Century Russian Literature

1

Russian Literature, 1900–1914

1   Chekhov: The Appreciator of Irony

At the beginning of the twentieth century, the great age of Russian literature seemed to lie in the past. Dostoyevsky had died in 1881, Turgenev two years later; and although Tolstoy lived until 1910, the important part of his writing career had long since passed.

The most significant Russian writer at the beginning of the new century, who was not at first recognized as such, was Anton Chekhov. A country doctor who became an author, he began publishing stories in the 1880s, turning toward the end of the century to writing plays for the Moscow Art Theater. There, Konstantin Stanislavsky produced Chekhov's most important dramas: *Chaika* (1896; *The Sea Gull*, literally *The Gull*), *Dyadya Vanya* (1899; *Uncle Vanya*), *Tri sestry* (1901; *The Three Sisters*), and *Vishnyovyi sad* (1904; *The Cherry Orchard*). Chekhov was only forty-four when he died of tuberculosis in 1904. (The age of forty-four seems a particularly fatal one for certain brilliant literary men, as in the cases of Spinoza, Stevenson, Thoreau, D. H. Lawrence, F. Scott Fitzgerald, and various others.)

Chekhov's short stories, often ruefully comic, revolutionized the medium. Instead of the well-made tale with its proper beginning, middle, and end, Chekhov presented ironic sketches full of insight and psychological surprise. The plays, which also had these qualities, are all the more remarkable because drama is so formally demanding: since the events, flashbacks and all, must unfold consecutively be-

1

fore an audience, plays are supposed to have an organic development; at least they were supposed to until Chekhov began writing them; that is, his dramas did not follow the canons of "form." He made it possible for playwrights to work outside the traditional expectation; his plays were often as plotless as his short stories.

Chekhov's writings, which suggest a broken world where few things are consecutive, reflect the days of the last tsar, when Russian morale had sagged; Chekhov's plays appeared on the eve of the 1904–5 war in which tiny Japan unexpectedly defeated the bulky Russian Empire. The plays themselves point the way to the 1917 revolution, not in any overt propagandistic way, but in their revelation of the apathy of the Russian upper and middle classes. Chekhov's dramas were for the most part concerned with the section of those classes known in Russia as the intelligentsia.

The Sea Gull is, with the plays of the Swedish author Strindberg, the true beginning of twentieth-century drama. Chekhov called *The Sea Gull* a comedy, even though its ending was as grim as that of Ibsen's *Hedda Gabbler*. The principal characters are essentially grotesque. They include Irina Arkadina (Madame Trepleva) and her paramour, Boris Trigorin, a literary man, as well as her son Konstantin and the girl he is in love with, Nina. Another girl, Masha, is in love with Konstantin. Nina, in turn, in the spirit of Chekhov's world, is in love with Trigorin, who doesn't notice her until she appears in a play by Konstantin, performed on his mother's estate.

This much occurs on the stage; offstage, Nina goes to Moscow as Trigorin's mistress, where she bears him a child that dies; and she is deserted by him. She returns to the country after an unsuccessful acting career, and still cannot fall in love with Konstantin, who has followed her everywhere. At the end of the play, the sound of a shot comes from offstage. Madame Arkadina is frightened, but everyone reassures her. Doctor Dorn goes to investigate and comes back quietly, falling into a discussion with Trigorin about an article in a magazine. As the play ends, he says to Trigorin in a low tone, "Get Irina Nikolayevna away somehow. The fact is, Konstantin Gavrilych has shot himself."

After finishing *The Sea Gull*, Chekhov wrote to his friend the newspaper editor, Aleksei Suvorin: "I began it forte and finished it pianissimo, against all the rules of dramatic art. It came out like a story. I am more dissatisfied than satisfied with it and, reading over my newborn piece, I become once more convinced that I am not a playwright at all." When the first performance was a fiasco, only one critic gave it a friendly review.

The play had been badly rehearsed, and the director had not understood it; despite the performances of several excellent actors, the audience had laughed in the wrong places and had whistled and shouted. (In European theaters, whistling is an equivalent of American booing.) But the play was revived in 1898 by the newly formed Moscow Art Theater, with Konstantin Stanislavsky as Trigorin, and then it was a lively success.

The following year, Chekhov permitted Stanislavsky to produce *Uncle Vanya*, which had been performed in some of the smaller towns of Russia. This play, which Chekhov subtitled "Scenes from Country Life," is another of those pictures of futility in which almost everyone seems to be in love with the least responsive person. Here the main character, Vanya, successfully manages an estate, chiefly for the benefit of the retired Professor Serebryakov, an indolent and self-centered old man with a beautiful wife, Yelena, aged twenty-seven. Vanya is in love with her, and so is the neighboring doctor, Astrov; while Sonya, the professor's daughter by his earlier wife, is hopelessly in love with Doctor Astrov. The only outward action of the play occurs when Vanya's patience with the professor runs out and he fires two shots at him. It is a measure of Vanya's futility that he misses both times. The doctor goes home, taking with him the morphine which Uncle Vanya had stolen from his bag; and the professor departs with the disturbing Yelena. Sonya assures her uncle at the end:

We shall go on living, Uncle Vanya! We shall live through a long, long chain of days and weary evenings; we shall patiently bear the trials which fate sends us; we shall work for others, both now and in our old age, and have no rest; and when our time comes we shall die without a murmur, and there beyond the grave we shall say that we have suffered, that we have wept, that life has been bitter to us, and God will have pity on us, and you and I, Uncle, dear Uncle, shall see a life that is bright, lovely, beautiful. We shall rejoice and look back at these troubles of ours with tenderness, with a smile—and we shall rest. I have faith, Uncle; I have fervent, passionate faith.

Chekhov, who because of his health had established residence in the south, at Yalta in the Crimea, was ill and fretful at the time of writing *The Three Sisters*. When he went to Moscow and first read it to the actors, he realized that they and the producers misunderstood his intention, and he even quarreled (mildly) with Stanislavsky. Nevertheless, the play was produced; it was not greeted with enthusiasm. It is the story of a trio of sisters and their brother in a garrison town; they are the children of the late brigadier. Throughout the play, the sisters keep speaking of their projected return to Moscow, which never materializes. A cry, "To Moscow! To Moscow!" hangs mockingly over the scene, and at the end of the piece the sisters are fastened as tightly as ever to their provincial town.

During the course of production of *The Three Sisters*, Chekhov married one of the actresses who was playing in it, Olga Knipper. He called his next and final play, *The Cherry Orchard*, a gay comedy, but Stanislavsky and the other Moscow players insisted it was a tragedy and performed it seriously. The result was successful enough, for the public took to the play. Stanislavsky and his fellow actors had apparently discovered the right tone for *The Cherry Orchard*, developing its nuances, its nostalgia, and its complex human relationships into a fine dramatic fabric.

The setting of the play is the country estate of Madame Ranevskaya, who returns from a long sojourn in France to realize that her Russian home must be sold because of the family debts. But she and her dreamy brother, Gayev, a compulsive billiard-player, are repelled by the suggestion made by Lopakhin, a well-to-do merchant whose father had been a serf, that the cherry orchard on the estate be cut down and turned into a resort area for summer cottagers. Impossible, Gayev and his sister cry: their cherry orchard is a famous one, mentioned in the *Encyclopedia*.

They do nothing as their debts mount, and when the estate is put up for auction, Mme. Ranevskaya gives a party. Lopakhin buys the estate and announces that he will cut down the cherry orchard. At the end of the play, the family leaves the old house, Mme. Ranevskaya heading for Paris, and as only the dying, ancient servant Firs is left on the stage, the sound of the axes chopping down the cherry trees can already be heard in the distance.

At the successful opening night of *The Cherry Orchard*, Chekhov appeared before the curtain to receive applause after the third and next-to-last act; he was so obviously ill that a member of the audience cried out for him to sit down. A few months later he went to Germany, where he died. His body was sent back to Moscow in a freight car used for the shipping of oysters. At the same station another coffin arrived bearing the body of a general killed in the Far East; those who had come to pay their respects to Chekhov followed the wrong coffin for a while and, when the mistake was discovered, smiled ruefully—it was the kind of irony that Chekhov would have appreciated.

His plays are still performed in Russia, and while also frequently produced elsewhere they are not always successful on the stage because of the special quality of underplaying they require. Even some of the world's finest classical actors are too accustomed to the heroic style to be able to adjust themselves to the Chekhovian tone. That quiet yet intense tone is still the perfect instrument of expression for the attitude of futility of the Russian intelligentsia and landed classes in the twilight of the tsars.

2   Gorky: The Lower Depths of Hope

The most prominent of Chekhov's contemporaries was Maxim Gorky, who was born Aleksei Peshkov in 1868, in Nizhni Novgorod, which is now called Gorky. Growing up along the Volga, Gorky in his youth engaged in many occupations which familiarized him with the lives of Russian agricultural workers, rivermen, and factory laborers. When he began writing stories in his twenties, he took the pseudonym Gorky, which means bitter.

A good part of his writing career belongs to the years after the First World War, to Soviet literature, and will be considered later. But Gorky wrote some of his most important books and plays in the early years of the twentieth century, indeed even before—in the decade of the nineties. His work from the first was characterized by intense realism and a hope of improving the human condition.

Chekhov wrote to Gorky, "You are an artist, a wise man . . . You feel superbly, you are plastic; that is, when you describe a thing you see it and touch it with your hands. That is real art." But Chekhov also spoke of Gorky's defects: "I shall begin by saying that, in my opinion, you do not use sufficient restraint. You are like a spectator in the theater who expresses his rapture so unreservedly that it prevents both himself and others from listening." And Lev Tolstoy said to Chekhov, "One can invent anything one likes, but one cannot invent psychology, and in Gorky one comes across psychological inventions; he describes what he has not felt."

These criticisms, coming from two great writers who saw the significance of Gorky's work from the first, apply to it across the years. There is no question that the prophetic strain in it, the propaganda, resulting in the false inventions that Tolstoy saw, is a handicap in the eyes of many present-day readers, although not in the Soviet Union, where Gorky is one of the gods in the literary pantheon.

Gorky's early novels, structureless and written in a style of violent impressionism, were at one level rallying cries for revolution: *Foma Gordeyev* (1899), *Troye* (1901; *Three of Them*), and *Mat'* (1907; *Mother*, also known as *The Comrades*). The last of these books was written in the Adirondack Mountains in New York, during Gorky's visit to America. He had been arrested during the 1905 uprisings, and there had even been a rumor that he was hanged. But he left Russia until the outbreak of the First World War because he was tubercular and needed a warm climate; he settled in Italy, at Sorrento and on the island of Capri. It was widely accepted in Russia that he was finished as a writer, so that in 1913 *Detstvo* (*My Childhood*), the first of his impressive autobiographical volumes, came as a distinct surprise. In 1914 he returned home, then from 1921 to 1928 again lived outside Russia, but he finally came back again.

Gorky's later career, as previously noted, belongs to Soviet literature. But the earlier *Na dne* (1902; *The Lower Depths*), is his most famous drama, still frequently revived. It was originally produced with great forcefulness by Stanislavsky's company, who went down to the actual setting, the Khitrov market quarter in Moscow, to become familiar with the speech and dress of the people there. The play is set in a broken-down lodging house, and the characters are a drunken ex-actor, a down-at-heel aristocrat, a prostitute, a thief, and others afflicted by various manifestations of poverty. But for all its documentation of the degraded (foreshadowing such plays as Eugene O'Neill's *The Iceman Cometh*), *The Lower Depths* has streaks of hope, particularly in the speeches of folk-philosopher, Luka, who has visions of paradise and declares that God exists if you believe in Him. "How can anybody cast off a human being?" Luka asks. "Whatever condition he's in, a human being is always worth something." A little later he explains, "I've been through the wringer—that's why I'm soft." There is some question as to whether Luka is really a savior or a fraud; Gorky ultimately tended toward the latter view.

3   Andreyev: The Sensationist of Despair

A writer who attracted almost as much attention as Gorky in the early twentieth century was Leonid Andreyev, author of the story "Krasny smekh" (1904; "The Red Laugh"), a hideous projection of war which underlined the feelings of a good many Russians at the time of the Japanese conflict. In another tale, "Rasskaz o semi poveshennykh" (1908; "The Seven Who Were Hanged"), Andreyev presented a psychological study of five political prisoners and two common criminals condemned to death. The story shows how each of them accepts the sentence and what his thoughts and feelings are between its pronouncement and the execution itself; and it shows the way in which they meet their deaths.

Andreyev was also a playwright. His first venture in this area, K zvyozdam (1906; To the Stars), would today be called an existentialist drama. In it an astronomer has withdrawn from the world to his observatory in the mountains, where he can ignore the revolution going on below in which his son is taking part. Zhizn' cheloveka (1907; The Life of Man), is an allegorical play, the story of Everyman, a pessimistic investigation of human existence. Andreyev's best-known drama, the one most often played outside Russia, Anatema (1909; Anathema), is a story of the devil's visit to the earth.

Eccentric, almost entirely sensational, Andreyev is no longer highly regarded, either in Russia or elsewhere. A supporter of the moderate Alexander Kerensky in the early phases of the 1917 revolution, he left the country because of his angry protest against the Bolsheviks. He went to Finland, where he died in 1919, apparently of hemorrhage of the brain.

4   Kuprin and Others

Alexander Kuprin was another contemporary of Gorky and Andreyev who attained great fame, particularly for his novel Poyedinok (1905; The Duel), full of brutal realism about army life, a book which caught the public fancy just after the Russian military defeats in the Japanese war. It was not intended as a revolutionary story, but it was taken by the left wing as an attack upon militarism. Kuprin had before the war served for several years as an officer and knew military life well. He scored another sensational success with *Yama* (1912; *Yama: The Pit*), an acidly realistic projection of life in a big-city brothel. Kuprin died of cancer in 1938, having recently returned to Russia after a number of years in Paris.

Sensationalism was what Russian readers seemed to want in those years before the First World War and the collapse of tsardom, the time of the Japanese war and the 1905 revolt. This appetite was gratified by the most famous book of Mikhail Artsybashev, his novel *Sanin* (1907), which recommended individual freedom in eroticism and other activities; many of the younger generation, to the horror of their elders, formed groups of Saninists.

On the other hand, there was a widespread response to the quieter novels and tales of Ivan Bunin who, in 1933, as an émigré, was to win the Nobel Prize. Bunin's most famous work was *Derevnya* (1910; *The Village*), a realistic picture of peasant life in Central Russia, a book which without being revolutionary is a convincing account of the darkness and misery of the lives of the peasants. Bunin's best-known story, "Gospodin iz San Frantsisko" (1916; "The Gentleman from San Francisco"), tells of the death of a rich American at Capri, whose body is ironically shipped back to America aboard the luxury steamer which had originally brought him; the gaiety of the members of the cruise is sharply contrasted with the coffin in the hold.

Another traditional writer of those years was Dmitry Merezhkovsky, author of the famous trilogy *Khristos i Antikhrist* (*Christ and the Antichrist*), consisting of *Smert' bogov* (1896; *Julian the Apostate*, also called *The Death of the Gods*), *Voskresshiye bogi: Leonardo da Vinci* (1901; *The Gods Resurrected*, translated as *The Romance of Leonardo da Vinci*), and *Pyotr i Aleksei* (1905; *Peter and Alexis*). These three books present the conflict between Christianity and paganism in three phases of history; they are too greatly weighed down by their philosophical content to have sufficient force as novels. Their sources were so well known that one critic called Merezhkovsky "the Napoleon of quotations."

Merezhkovsky, who was perhaps better as a critic than as

a novelist, has left illuminating commentaries in such studies as *Tolstoy i Dostoyevsky* (1901; *Tolstoy as Man and Artist, with an Essay on Dostoyevsky*). Merezhkovsky was not, however, in a class with two of the influential philosophical essayists of the day, Vasily Rozanov and Lev Shestov, both of whom were later to interest D. H. Lawrence.

5 Pre-Soviet Poets

The poets Blok and Mayakovsky, who were writing at this time, will be considered under the category of Soviet literature. But two other poets may be mentioned at this point: Fyodor Sologub (1863–1927), who stayed in Russia after the revolution but remained aloof from it until his death, and Aleksei Remizov (1877–1957), who became an émigré. Both these men, originally identified with the Symbolists, became better known for their novels than for their poems.

Sologub was born Fyodor Teternikov; his best-known novel, *Melkiy bes* (1907; *The Little Demon*), is both satiric and symbolic; its hero, Peredonov, a paranoid schoolmaster, gave Russians a new name for pettiness and baseness—Peredonovism. *The Little Demon*, which Sologub began writing in serial form in the nineties, has a horribly realistic ending, with Peredonov as a murderer. *Tvorimaya legenda* (1908–12; *Created Legend*) is a series of novels about a satanic magician, typical of the figures which occur throughout Sologub's poems and stories.

Remizov's poems and fiction were likewise full of devils, hobgoblins, and ghosts. His novels, including *Pyataya yazva* (1912; *The Fifth Pestilence*), frequently express the author's distaste for town living as against country existence. Remizov was a sharp stylist who often wrote in the vein of folklore; he carried on Nikolai Leskov's tradition of *skaz*, an attempt to reproduce the exact idiom of each speaker in a story. Although Remizov left Russia in 1921 and remained in exile until his death in 1957, he was a strong influence upon Soviet writers of the neorealist school.

The period between 1900 and the First World War is often called the Silver Age of Russian literature. In contradistinction to the Golden Age of the nineteenth century, which was mostly that of classical prose, the Silver Age was mainly that of exquisite poetry, populated by such imposing schools as the Symbolists, the Acmeists, and others. The Symbolists believed in abstract metaphysical symbols as the world's reality, in art for art's sake. They stressed mysticism and eroticism; they advocated and practiced a fine musicality of rhythms and forms in their writings, particularly in poetry. The Acmeists opposed the mystic, transcendental quality of the Symbolists who, they argued, were too unclear, too labored, too misty while being mystic. The Acmeists strove toward the highest level ("the acme") of the natural in contrast to man's social or artificial essence. While seeking the sensuous, they differed from the Symbolists in searching for a flexible clarity of the artistic image and the poetical language.

In addition to the already discussed Merezhkovsky, Sologub, and Remizov, there were: Andrei Bely (1880–1934), Alexander Blok (1880–1921), Nikolai Gumilyov (1886–1921), Valery Bryusov (1873–1924), Konstantin Balmont (1867–1943), Vladislav Khodasevich (1886–1939), and Vyacheslav Ivanov (1866–1949). Two magazines, *Vesy* (*Balance*) and *Vekhi* (*Landmarks*), were outstanding as rallying points of these and other poets, short-story writers, and essayists. At Ivanov's lodgings in St. Petersburg, nicknamed "The Tower," gatherings were regularly held at which the latest poems were read, and discoveries of fresh talents made. Ivanov was one of the very first to recognize the great talent of Anna Akhmatova (1888–1966), Gumilyov's young wife, among his other discoveries. A notable literary salon was presided over by Zinaida Hippius (sometimes spelled Gippius; 1867–1945), Merezhkovsky's wife and a Symbolist poet and essayist in her own right.

The guns of August 1914 did not at first seem to make much change in the style and substance of the Silver Age poets: they went on, or tried to go on, with their moods and meters. Russia had helped bring on that war, though her foreign minister, Sergei Sazonov, tried to avert conflict in July 1914 by requesting Austria to modify her demands on Serbia. Austria, backed by Germany, would not do so, and Russia, sponsoring Serbia, refused to demobilize when the German emperor demanded this. If Russia had capitulated, the German-Austrian alliance would have been dominant in Europe—in short, the Russian decision was a complicated one, both good and bad, as most such decisions prove to be in the modern world. So the Russians stayed in battle order, and the Germans began moving against them and, in the other direction, against the Belgians; the world was at war.

Several of the Silver Age poets and essayists were at first duly—and a few even belligerently—patriotic. But with the war dragging on, and the nation becoming tired and disillusioned, the poets endeavored to return to their old, peaceful themes. The revolution, made possible by Russia's collapse toward the end of the First World War, was initially hailed by the poets and other writers. But the Bolshevik takeover dispirited most of them. Some writers became émigrés, others stayed, but the lives and work of all were changed by the revolution.

Most of the twentieth-century Russian authors not yet presented in this narrative will be discussed in our chapters devoted to the time since the revolution of 1917.

2

Soviet Literature to the Second World War

1   Beginnings in a Red Dawn: Bely, Blok, Yesenin, Mayakovsky

The Russian upheaval of 1917 was no exception to the rule that periods of revolution can stimulate literature. After the first excitement, however, this revolution settled down to become authoritarian; and literature, like the other arts, was often in difficulty, though writers went on writing, many of them very well. Today, particularly after the treatment of Boris Pasternak for producing *Doktor Zhivago*, with subsequent attitudes toward other authors, such as Alexander Solzhenitsyn, the world knows how hard it is to be a writer in Russia, though the authors who find it possible to conform are given abundant rewards. The Mikhail Zoshchenko case was an earlier example than Pasternak's of the fate of the nonconformist; like his, it will be discussed later.

The Russian revolution of 1917, like most drastic social revolutions (in which the people's way of life is changed) was not at first extensively violent, in the image of Hollywood extras with improvised weapons storming the palace; rather, in the tradition of authentic revolutions, the Russian upheaval was for the most part a matter of abdication and committee, and of several generations of readiness. The tsar, Nicholas II, had crushed the "Red Sunday" revolt of 1905; but the mood of the country, particularly after the unexpected defeats of the imperial navy by Japan, induced him to call a *duma*, or parliament, in 1906. This and its successor in 1907 were violently antigovernment and were dissolved; the last two *dumas*, from 1907 to 1912 and from 1912 to the war, were mostly centrist and not too unfriendly to the government. In 1917, with the nation unable to sustain the

13

burden of the war, the government collapsed from within, and the tsar abdicated. The succeeding Provisional Government of Alexander Kerensky, representing a rather nervous bourgeois liberalism, soon fell apart, and Vladimir Lenin and his organized Bolsheviks took over—Lenin, an exile from Russia, had been financed by the Germans in the hope that he would create dissension.

Lenin's platform was a demand for the end of Russian participation in the war, for the control of the means of production by the workers, and for seizure of the estates of the aristocrats. The upper and some of the middle classes fought back—and the violence of revolutions is in the civil wars brought on by those who have already lost their controls—until Lev Trotsky's forces defeated the last White armies under Baron Pyotr Wrangel in 1920. Then the Soviet state firmly established itself. All these were events which have had an emphatic influence on the literature of our time.

Let us set down these few general considerations: A totalitarian government controls or tries to control the arts of the nation it rules. Literature, painting and sculpture, theater and opera, ballet, music, films—all these are an important area of dictatorial repression and a valuable tool of propaganda. This is all true of the Soviet régime which from its beginnings to these days has always been a totalitarian system.

Long before coming to power Lenin had considered and forecast the role the arts should play once his Party took over. From its very inception in 1917 his Soviet government devised measures to supervise, suppress, and use the arts. Under Joseph Stalin, from the latter 1920s to his death in 1953, the arts of all the peoples in the Soviet empire, Russian and non-Russian, underwent an increasingly decisive surgical operation by censorship and outright orders to write, paint, and compose in certain ways and no others. After Stalin, at short intervals of Khrushchevian permissiveness, there were outbursts of freewheeling creativeness, but these did not last. In this post-Khrushchev period arts-by-decree are once more a sad fact, although not so devastatingly as they were in the pitch-black night of Stalin's reign.

State censorship of literature, theater, and other arts continues to exist most thoroughly, although officially its fact is acknowledged but minimally. Even in dictionaries and encyclopedias the very word *tsenzura* or censorship is meant for capitalistic countries or when referring to the old tsarist times, never in regard to the present-day Soviet censorship. The official article on censorship in volume 46 of the *Great Soviet Encyclopedia* (1957) devotes more than one full page to Western and tsarist censorship, but barely admits and then most self-righteously describes Soviet censorship as something entirely moral and necessary at the very end of the article, in just two brief paragraphs.

A network of special censorship offices has been developed by the Party and its government for various purposes, areas, fields, and specialties of human expression, but the most general and mighty Soviet state office of censorship is the so-called *Glavlit*, the telescoped word for *Glavnoye upravleniye po delam literatury i izdatel'stv*, or Main Office on Matters of Literature and Publishing Houses, more recently renamed *Glavnoye upravleniye po okhrane voyennykh i gosudarstvennykh tain v pechati*, or Main Office of Safeguarding Military and State Secrets in the Press.

In their domination over the arts the Communist Party and its Soviet government have been motivated by three premises. In the order of their importance these are: First, while censoring any truly free expression, to use the arts as a medium of propaganda, so as to cause the population to do this or that within the Party's program for the nation, to support the Soviet government actively in this current or long-range policy or that.

Second, to use the arts as a distracting, dulling, pacifying agency—to make the populace forget their plentiful troubles. This is the ancient bread-and-circus idea, of course: if there isn't enough bread—of tangible, material things of life—for the people, there is always the circus.

Third, to display a degree of genuine concern for the enlightenment of the masses. Naturally, Soviet propagandists insist that this is the first, foremost, and only aim of the Party and the government in their use of the arts. But most of the world by now knows that it is the least viable—a very distant third—of the three considerations.

To sum up the effect of the Soviet control of the arts: The positive side is that the masses are now given a wider, freer access to the arts than they perhaps were in prerevolutionary times. The overwhelmingly negative feature is that the arts are manipulated to such an appalling extent that often they cease being arts; and that if the arts are employed as a complement to terror it may indeed be better if there were no arts at all.

In the initial battle-filled period of the Soviet régime, creative writers wrote but hardly published, for, as the civil war raged, the opposing forces—the Reds and the Whites—used their printing presses and the scarce reserves of paper to extol their causes and for other militant journalism, not for nonpolitical novels, stories, and poetry. As chaos and starvation plagued the nation, the reader sought forgetfulness in old classics, not in whatever little new was then published.

Painters and sculptors lacked paints and clay; actors, composers, and musicians were either silent and unemployed or performed in half-empty theaters and halls.

Death from bullets or hunger came to some practitioners of arts when it struck down indiscriminately many other Russians of all classes and professions. A shocking loss was the execution by a Red firing squad in 1921 of Nikolai Gumilyov, thirty-seven years old, one of Russia's most talented poets founding and heading the Acmeist group. The charge was participation in an anti-Soviet conspiracy.

With the millions of middle- and upper-class Russians fleeing to foreign lands there migrated, some for good, others not, the writers Ivan Bunin, Alexander Kuprin, Maxim Gorky, Aleksei Tolstoy, Dmitry Merezhkovsky and his wife Zinaida Hippius, also Ilya Ehrenburg, Boris Zaitsev, Vladislav Khodasevich, and—as yet a teen-ager, but already then holding the promise of his extraordinary gift—Vladimir Nabokov. They left because they were hostile to the Communists. The composers Igor Stravinsky, Sergei Prokofyev, Sergei Rachmaninov, and later Alexander Glazunov became émigrés. So did Fyodor Chaliapin, the singer, as well as Anna Pavlova and Sergei Diaghilev of the ballet.

When the civil war ended with the Red victory, however, and Lenin introduced the breathing spell of the New Economic Policy, the early and middle 1920s were marked at home by a sudden, tumultous blossoming of all the arts. To explain this NEP or the New Economic Policy, with its new outlook: Industry was in a state of ruin at the close of the civil war, and agriculture was lagging in a time of drought, with the result that there was famine across the land. Lenin's NEP attempted to stimulate the economy by permitting a limited return to capitalism. Although the government kept control of banks, heavy industries, transportation and foreign trade, small plants operated under private ownership, food levies were abolished, and the currency system was stabilized. This policy, which lasted into 1928, brought about greater freedom in social and literary manifestations.

Hence the 1920s proved to be a relatively untrammeled period in Soviet history. Literature in particular experienced a revival. Some Russians wrote with hope in their hearts for a new freedom. It was chiefly poetry that they produced at first; good, or even readable, prose came somewhat later, as did the era's better plays.

Many writers did not migrate to foreign lands, but stayed in Russia to accept or in some cases even to celebrate the revolution. Among these were notably Alexander Blok, Andrei Bely, Isaac Babel, Boris Pilnyak, Sergei Yesenin, and Vladimir Mayakovsky. The last two ended as suicides.

Private publishing was permitted in the NEP period, and an astonishingly lively and imaginative variety of imprints appeared in Moscow. A limited contact with Russian émigré writers and publishers in the West was allowed. A few émigré authors were taking positions on the left and even returning. Most strikingly, Ehrenburg, until then a vigorous anti-Communist, in 1923 became the European correspondent of the Moscow *Izvestiya*, the Soviet government's main official newspaper. Several years later, after a number of visits to the Soviet Union, he stayed there. It was also in 1923 that Aleksei Tolstoy came back from Western Europe, to his new influence and affluence as a Soviet propagandist. Maxim Gorky lived and wrote in Germany and Italy from 1921 until 1928, in which year he came back to support

Stalin's policies—only to become disillusioned, and to die disconsolate in 1936. Kuprin returned from the West a broken man, to die in 1938. (Among the composers, Prokofyev came back—to die in early March 1953, almost on the same day as Stalin. But Stravinsky returned many years later, on a triumphant visit, though not to stay.)

The gamut of styles and views ranged from Vladimir Mayakovsky, in his poetry and posters thunderously singing the glories of Communism; through the semi-sympathetic, semi-critical attitudes of such "fellow travelers" in Soviet fiction as Boris Pilnyak and Isaac Babel with their taut prose and Osip Mandelshtam with his fathomless poetry; to Sergei Yesenin's open disagreement with the Party in his now bold, now gentle lyrics. And side by side with these new and young idols of the youth, the older Symbolists such as Alexander Blok, Valery Bryusov, and Andrei Bely, supporting the Soviet régime in varying degrees but on the whole rather lukewarmly, continued their sway over new poetry, as also—Bely, in particular—over prose.

Of the poets, Bely and Blok belonged to the prewar Russian Symbolist movement; Mayakovsky was a Futurist, and the peasant Yesenin, whose work was chiefly postwar, was associated with the Imaginists, who called themselves the successors of the Futurists.

The pseudonymous last name of Bely means white: he was born in 1880, as Boris Bugayev, son of a noted mathematics professor at the University of Moscow. In his youth he became one of the editors of the Symbolist magazine Vesy (Balance), but by 1912 had gone over to the anthroposophical school of Rudolf Steiner. After a long sojourn abroad, Bely returned to Russia in time for the revolution, which he hailed with messianic outbursts; he was now briefly one of the Scythians, who confronted the new social events with fervor and a sense of exultation. In 1922, Bely left Russia to live in Berlin, but returned the following year, and until his death in 1934 remained one of Soviet Russia's most interesting authors, taking part—not too enthusiastically—in many of the new nation's cultural activities. His work—essentially bourgeois, Symbolist, and experimental—has not had a lasting influence in his homeland, although in the years after the revolution it exerted an influence upon Boris Pilnyak and others.

In addition to his poetry, Bely wrote what is generally regarded as some of the finest Russian prose of this century. His novels include *Serebryanyi golub'* (1910; *The Silver Dove*), *Peterburg* (written in 1910–11, first published in 1913; *St. Petersburg*), both in the vein of grotesquery found in Gogol and sometimes in Dostoyevsky. In 1922, Bely brought out his autobiographical short novel, *Kotik Letayev*, which in its passages dealing with the development of a child's consciousness recalls both Joyce and Proust. Toward the end of his life Bely published several reminiscential volumes, in the vein of an earlier one he had written about Alexander Blok, whom the world outside Russia esteems far more than it does Bely. *St. Petersburg* was the first of his novels to be published in English (New York, 1959; London, 1960).

Born in the same year as Bely, 1880, Blok began publishing poems when he was twenty. His *Stikhi o prekrasnoi dame* (1904; *Verses about the Beautiful Lady*), a Dante-like address to a figure that was at once a woman and Sophia, or Divine Wisdom, drew upon Symbolist method in its half-mystical evocations. In the years immediately following, Blok intensified his allegiance to the Symbolists, though he also had ties with romanticism. When the First World War came he saw it as an apocalyptic beginning of a new life that would have to come through destruction; the war itself he vigorously opposed, though he was eventually compelled to serve in it. He welcomed the revolution and wrote his finest poem about it—"Dvenadtsat'" (1918; "The Twelve").

The title may suggest the disciples of Christ, if only in a parodic way; and Christ also seems to appear in the poem, walking ahead of the twelve revolutionary soldiers who are being fired at as they patrol the icy streets of Petrograd. It is not clear whether Christ is actually leading them, or whether he is again a martyr. The poem, in twelve long sections, begins:

> *White the snow*
> *Black the night*

> Wind, wind!
> No man can keep his feet,
> Wind, wind—
> Over all God's world it blows!

Even those who cannot read Russian can feel the force of this in the original:

> Chyornyi vecher
> Belyi sneg
> Veter, veter!
> Na nogahk ne stoit chelovek.
> Veter, veter—
> Na vsyem bozhyem svete!

As the group stamps on, one of their former comrades, Van'ka, passes in a sledge with his girl Katya; one of the twelve fires at them and kills Katya. The patrol continues its march, the murderer feeling remorse, crying out his guilt. The storm intensifies. "The Twelve" ends:

> Forward they go commandingly,
> A starving cur behind them,
> A blood-red banner in advance:
> Unseen in blinding snow,
> Unharmed by flying bullets,
> And walking softly through the storm
> Of tossing, pearly flakes,
> And crowned with roses, Christ
> Marches before them by himself.

With its vivid images and its crowning ambiguity, "The Twelve" represents an application of the Symbolist and romantic attitudes to harsh political events of the moment. But Blok's writing career was at an end; in the same month as he composed "The Twelve" (January 1918) he wrote "Skify" ("The Scythians"), and that was all. "The Scythians" is an Asiatic cry of defiance to the Western nations: sympathize with us and work together with us or we will sweep down in Scythian hordes upon your decaying cultures.

By the summer of 1921, Blok had burned himself out; he

died of an asthmatic and cardiac condition, in a state of
nervous exhaustion and delirium. Toward the last, he wrote
in diary notes of his love and hatred of the vile Mother
Russia that was devouring him. Those were hard years in
which to be a poet. Pasternak, often criticized by the orthodox for his aloofness, survived as man and writer to the
age of seventy; as noted earlier, Yesenin and Mayakovsky
were suicides.

Sergei Yesenin, when inflamed by the revolution, wrote
poems fervent with orthodox religious symbols. As a member
of the so-called Imaginist group after 1919, Yesenin belonged
to the post-Symbolist, post-Futurist vanguard which was the
only organized school in the years immediately following the
revolution. In technique these writers had much in common
with the Anglo-American imagists, in their sharp focus upon
the visually concrete, but in outlook they were different in
that they flaunted a pessimistic and morbid attitude.

Yesenin, one of whose marriages was to the American
dancer Isadora Duncan, became a bohemian and a nightclub
figure, all the while pathetically seeing himself as a François
Villon craving to associate with the lawless. Yesenin became
a drunkard and at times was hospitalized after his bouts, but
his poetry continued to be forceful. This is particularly true
of *Moskva kabatskaya* (1924; *Tavern Moscow*), in whose
title poem he speaks of having forsaken the fields and trees
of his home background, as decreed by God "on the twisted
Moscow streets," which the poet loves in all their muddiness
—for, on the golden domes above those streets, Asia herself
sleeps. All night in taverns the poet reads his verses to
whores, while back home his peasant hut falls apart. As
guitar and accordion play, he celebrates the loves of a flashing moment, but asserts that he will never die.

Alas for such hopes: Yesenin at Christmastime 1925, when
he was thirty years old, slashed his wrists in a hotel room and,
after writing his last poem in his own blood, hanged himself
in his bitterness—and perhaps his poetic prevision of the
worse times yet to come. But in spite of this antirevolutionary
act, his verse continued to be popular in Russia. The émigré
Bunin called Yesenin "a sentimental hooligan," and the

22   TWENTIETH-CENTURY RUSSIAN LITERATURE

Party-line critics often frowned on his work, but it has re-mained in print and is still widely read. When in the sum-mer of 1973 a new two-volume edition of Yesenin's poetry was announced by the State Publishing House for an early printing, two million Soviet readers ready with their rubles signed up for what they considered a welcome treat.

Something of the same may be said of Vladimir Mayakov-sky who, in broken lines—half verse, half telegraphese—wrote at first the poetry of Futurism. Mayakovsky, who had spent his early childhood in the Transcaucasian province of Georgia, was taken in adolescence to Moscow, where he went to school. At nineteen he was one of the ardent signers of the Futurist manifesto, *Poshchyochina obshchesteven-nomu vkusu* (*A Slap in the Face of Public Taste*). His nota-ble poem of 1915, "Oblako v shtanakh" ("The Cloud in Trousers"), combined social exhortation with the romantic individualism of the grotesquely disappointed lover. At some levels—not only in the spasmodically arranged lines but in mischievousness and wit—Mayakovsky resembled the Amer-ican poet, E. E. Cummings, who a few years later began his attacks on typography and wrote his satires on idealism.

The prerevolutionary Mayakovsky merely satirized the hated bourgeoisie; after the Bolshevik success, the Futurist movement collapsed, but Mayakovsky continued writing in a somewhat Futurist manner, though now his subject matter changed: he composed poems about taxes, machines, the New Economic Policy, current history, food prices, and similar topics. With the coming of the new régime, he at last had something to believe in, and he poured his fervor into these social poems. He called himself the "drummer" of the revolution.

But disillusion set in. His prose plays, *Klop* (1928; *The Bedbug*) and *Banya* (1930; *The Bathhouse*), satirized the new philistinism of the Soviet Union and the growth of bureaucracy. In 1930, when he was thirty-seven, Mayakovsky, who had reprimanded Yesenin for his unrevolutionary deed in surrendering to despair and killing himself, also became a suicide. It is impossible to say how great a role his disap-pointment in the revolution played in driving him to shoot himself; he was ill, and like the pathetically ridiculous figure in "The Cloud in Trousers," he was the victim of un-requited love. Whatever the cause, illness was the official explanation, and Mayakovsky has in later times been re-garded in Russia as the supreme poet of the revolution.

Yet, the last few years of his life had been made difficult for him by the Party's literary hacks who (apparently on Stalin's orders) denounced him as not revolutionary enough, the lickspittles carrying on a shocking campaign of harass-ment and insults against this remarkable poet.

2   Control of the Arts: Commissar as Censor

It is now time to look at some of the movements and organizations that attempted to control the arts in the early years of the revolution. *Control* is the key word here, for that is what the state began to impose upon the arts as soon as it became firmly established.

Some of the leading Soviet writers and artists accepted dictation without complaint; others of course opposed it, though even in those early days it was not usually safe to do so openly. Oddly enough, some West European liberals out-side Russia—the type of people usually against legislation of art—generally supported the restrictions upon it because the state was new and needed encouragement. This attitude, embodying the often perilously necessary tolerance so im-portant in the history of liberalism, is an attitude which liberals for the most part no longer maintain.

Nevertheless, the Soviet state has produced much art that has been admired in Western nations. Earlier it was the Russian films, particularly those of Sergei Eisenstein, such as *Potemkin*; today it is the Russian ballet or an occasional solo performer of music on the violin or the piano. But critics, musicians, and authors remember the experiences of such composers as Dmitry Shostakovich and Aram Khachaturian in the 1930s and '40s, who were commanded to stop writing Western-like "bourgeois music," and the somewhat parallel vexations of Mikhail Zoshchenko, Boris Pasternak, Alexander Solzhenitsyn, and other later writers.

In Russia the techniques of mass persuasion, and attitudes

toward all the arts, were being debated by hot-faced men in committees who made decisions that were carried out coldly. After the revolution, a group of writers announced the birth of proletarian culture. The magazine *Proletarskaya kul'tura* incorporated the name of the movement, which itself became, in shorthand, *Proletkul't*. The leading spirit of the group and the journal was the critic A. Bogdanov (pseudonym of Alexander Malinovsky) who, at the first *Proletkul't's* congress in 1918, offered a resolution to the effect that the new society needed its own "class art." This resolution was carried unanimously.

The *Proletkul't*, which attempted to maintain its independence of political control, set up hundreds of workshops throughout Russia, in which leading writers taught. But these attempts at artificial inspiration didn't produce anything forcefully new in the way of literature. After the civil war ended in 1921, Lenin, who could then turn his annoyed attention to this too-individualistic movement of "Bogdanovism," placed the *Proletkul't* under the direction of the Commissariat of Education. Officially the *Proletkul't* ceased its existence in 1922. Within the next few years the movement had fizzled out, but the residue of some of its ideas influenced future attempts to set up a proletarian culture. Bogdanov died in 1928.

Meanwhile, Mayakovsky and the Futurists had adapted their techniques and interests to authoritarianism of LEF, the left-front literary group, which at first supported the extremist *Napostovtsy*, or On Guardists. Their magazines were *Oktyabr'* (*October*), founded 1923, and *Na postu* (*On Guard*), founded 1924. Before long the On Guardists were attacking LEF and were themselves coming under attack by the moderate critic, Alexander Voronsky, who edited *Krasnaya nov'* (*Red Virgin Soil*), founded 1921, the first important Soviet monthly magazine.

One group of writers formed at this time was the *Serapionovy bratya* [Serapion Brothers], who took their name from the hermit Serapion, an advocate of freedom of the creative imagination in one of the *Tales* of the romantic German writer E. T. A. Hoffman. The Serapions were not hostile to the revolution, but they were often satirical

(Zoshchenko was one of them), and they didn't stress propaganda. Their first *Al'manakh* (*Almanac*) 1922, marked a new frontier in Soviet prose literature.

In his book *Literature and Revolution* (1923), Trotsky placed the Serapions among the *poputchiki*, or fellow travelers. This term gave status to the writers who, while not officially Communists, went along with the revolution and opposed its enemies. This comparative freedom, which was a triumph over the fierce authoritarianism of the On Guardists, lasted almost until the end of the 1920s, when Stalin's First Five-Year Plan brought back rigorous controls.

Two other groups besides the Serapions which flourished in the 1920s were the Constructivists and the Formalists. The former were less important; founded in 1924, they were related to the Futurists, and although they celebrated technology and other themes of the moment, they were less antitraditional than the Futurists. To these Constructivists, theme was more important than language; they tried to establish an art of writing that would be functional in a collective society. The Formalists, originally related to the Symbolists, dated from the First World War. In criticism they denied the value of the sociological and other such background material, in a spirit similar to that of the purists among the later "new critics" in America. In creative work, the Soviet Formalists stressed the value of presenting the ordinary in extraordinary ways; their emphasis was on techniques. These Formalists remained strong through the 1920s; they were staunchly denounced in the next decade, by which time the other group, the Constructivists, had collapsed.

It was then, in the later twenties, with the end of the NEP and the beginning of forced industrialization and collectivization, that the short-lived freedom of Russian arts died. Neither the *Proletkul't*'s activity, nor the efforts of other would-be proletarian writers and artists in the NEP time, had seriously interfered with the relative independence of the fellow travelers and other non-Communist men and women of arts. But with the NEP's end, the Party opened a drive against intellectual liberty in earnest.

Private publishing was forbidden. Even cooperative bookstores run by groups of writers and other intellectuals were closed. Everything was to be handled by the state only. Librarians were admonished, their rights of choosing books diminished, and their professional associations censored. From 1928 and '29 on, increasingly harsh ukases came from the Party, ordering everybody to behave, and all writers had to do what was good for the Soviet state and no other cause, no matter how artistic, neutral, and otherwise nonpolitical. In 1928, a special organization, RAPP, the Russian initials standing for the Russian Association of Proletarian Writers, was set up and unleashed against would-be nonconformists, all this under the thinly veiled auspices of the secret police.

From then on, throughout most of the Stalinist reign, fear and submission prevailed in the Soviet arts. In fiction, poetry, drama, literary criticism, as well as in painting, sculpture, theater, and films the official rules of the so-called Socialist realism had to be adhered to, which meant that only slicked-up plots and tableaux of Soviet life, only praise for industrialization, collectivization, and extreme national-ism and chauvinism, but, above all, for the Communist Party and its Great Leader Stalin had to be presented. Not human life and love, but the needs of the Party, the Leader, and the state were to be praised. A bitter jest was whispered that a typical plot ran as follows: Boy meets tractor, boy falls in love with tractor, boy marries tractor, and they live hap-pily ever after for the weal of the Party, the Leader, and the Socialist State, driving that tractor toward the Communist society of the radiant tomorrow.

Another would-be-free writers' group which did not last was that of *Pereval* (*Mountain Pass*), founded in 1924. It attracted several peasant writers, as well as various Com-munist authors in good standing, but it was ferociously at-tacked by the Party orthodox because of its elements of in-dependence. The *Pereval* writers became associated with the journal *Krasnaya nov'*.

Its editor, Alexander Voronsky, was evidently exiled to Siberia after being thrown out of the Party as a Trotskyist at the instigation of Leopold Averbakh who, as head of RAPP, became dictator of Soviet literature. Voronsky was permitted to return in 1930 after a recantation, but in a few years he disappeared altogether, dying in prison in 1943. Averbakh himself was also arrested and also died in prison, in 1939. The *Pereval* group, which dissolved in 1932, was later designated as having been Trotskyite at the time when Lev Trotsky was a much-hated and voluble exile. One of the most notable productions of *Pereval* was the novel *Moloko* (1930; *Milk*), by Ivan Katayev (not related to the Katayev brothers, Valentin and Yevgeny); officially, *Milk* was accused of being too sentimentally bourgeois in its treatment of Soviet themes.

Not all of the goals of the First Five-Year Plan were achieved by the time it ended in 1932, but industry was expanded and collectivization carried out in farms and villages. The regimentation that these activities involved spread into literature. The Stalinist (and anti-Trotskyist) policy, which concentrated upon the firm establishment of Socialism in one country before encouraging it strongly in others, had begun to express itself in literature through RAPP, whose doctrine was *sotsial'ny zakaz*, or social command, through which all authors were now compelled to submit to the Party line. (The Russian word *zakaz* actually means an order, an assignment.) The dominance of RAPP and its policies choked the new literature that had begun to thrive under the NEP's mild liberalism.

The RAPP dictatorship over authors came to an end in 1932. The Communist Party's Central Committee dissolved the organization, which had brought about the imprisonment, banishment, or ostracism of writers who refused to conform. Now that the idea of *sotsialisticheskiy realizm*, or Socialist realism, succeeded that of social command, a single Union of Soviet Writers took the place of RAPP. Maxim Gorky became the first president of the new organization.

On the surface, at least, its principles were far more liberal than those of RAPP. It included writers of all beliefs, so that there were no more separate groups such as proletarians and fellow travelers, and nominally it restored some of the freedom of expression of the 1920s. Nevertheless, this new organization implicitly forbade any strong display of heresy; agreement with the goals of the revolution, as defined by the Party, was intimated in its pronunciamentos. In 1934, for example, in *Literature of the Peoples of the USSR* (nos. 7 and 8 of the V*oks Illustrated Almanac*), the critic Valery Kirpotin said, in an article on Socialist realism:

> The overwhelming majority of Soviet writers are striving with their works to help in the building of a new society. Its ties with the working class and with great ideas of Socialism have given Soviet literature a profound vitality. In contrast with pre-revolutionary literature, our literature is characterized by a deep organic connection with life. The best Soviet writers pride themselves on the fact that in their work they express the ardent dreams of millions of workers and peasants, their struggle, and the results of their victories. Soviet literature is unusually thirsty for life; it ceaselessly watches life, and learns from it. The best Soviet writers would be ashamed to write on a theme that was not of a social character, or on a theme that they had not studied.

Such utterances went beyond Russia and rang through the Western nations during the depression: they were taken up by the previously mentioned liberal intellectuals, who became fervent about "a theme they had not studied" and who very often knew nothing about workers and farmers or their struggles. These enthusiasts for the faraway missed the threats hidden in such phrases as "the overwhelming majority" or the ambiguous classification of "the best Soviet writers." Outsiders failed to understand that such wordage often disguised the obliteration of minority rights which so many of those same intellectuals fought for, or believed they were fighting for, in the democracies. In Russia the situation wasn't easy for those who didn't belong to the overwhelming majority; and even those who did belong to it, and were ranked among the "best" writers, had to be instructed, in this definition of Socialist realism, as to what should make them ashamed.

And yet conditions for some writers and other artists improved at least slightly under the new Union. This organization carried on, with some modifications, through the Second World War and on into the present epoch. During that last conflict, known in Russia as the Great Patriotic War, there was little enough trouble aside from the German attack, but in the subsequent epoch of peace the Writers' Union itself was accused of backsliding by the Party's Central Committee, and further abrogations of freedom were made.

After the death of Vladimir Lenin in 1924, Joseph Stalin by clever and ruthless degrees became head of the state; his rival, Lev Trotsky, lost his power in the Party in 1926 and was banished from the USSR three years later. But he carried on ideological opposition to Stalin and his Socialism-in-one-country claim, and throughout the world he attracted many followers. Within the Soviet Union, support of Trotsky was regarded as one of the worst deviations from the political norm, and incurred stringent punishments. Trotsky, who lived in a stronghold in a Mexico City suburb, was murdered there, on August 20, 1940, on Stalin's orders, by a dedicated Stalinist fanatic, a young Spanish Communist, who slipped inside the house and brained Trotsky with an alpinist's ax.

Russia shook in the late 1930s under the impact of the Moscow trials, set off by the assassination, on December 1, 1934, of Stalin's close associate, Sergei Kirov. In the trials and in the resultant purges, many former Party leaders and prominent generals were brought into court and ordered to be executed or imprisoned. Some of them were accused of working with Trotsky, some with the Nazis, and yet others with both; the trials, some held in public, but many behind closed doors, attracted worldwide interest.

For the first time the Soviet legal system—in which the accused is presumed guilty when brought into the courtroom —could be examined by outsiders. The United States Ambassador Joseph E. Davies, who was a lawyer, found nothing wrong with the trials; neither did Bernard Shaw's friends, the old Fabians Beatrice and Sydney Webb (the latter had accepted the title Lord Passfield, but his wife refused to be called milady). Most Western newspapers were unfriendly in their reports of the trials, and from the start there was something puzzling about them: the prisoners eagerly confessed to treasonable behavior and accused themselves with the fervor of Dostoyevskian characters. The outside world, most of whose inhabitants were not readers of Dostoyevsky, was little acquainted with the Russian temperament, and whatever techniques of brainwashing had been developed by Soviet officials were still a local secret. But Western democratic opinion, never strongly favorable to the Soviet Union, was turned vigorously against it during the Moscow trials.

The toll of the purges in those terrible thirties included many men and women of the arts, most notably of letters. Later, adding also the victims of the forties and early fifties, Alexander Solzhenitsyn estimated that some six hundred Russian writers were murdered by the Stalinist executioners and slave drivers.

And yet, as a mocking refrain of this bloodbath, the Party message was repeated again and again that Soviet writers were as valuable to the new state as engineers, that (in Stalin's dull phrase) they were "engineers of the human soul." This meant the same old "Socialist realism" and its lie-ridden shibboleths. And so, emitting their pious cant, many bootlickers continued to prosper.

Some of the toadies were not without talent. Mikhail Sholokhov's novels and stories of life and war in the Don steppes showed genuine perception, yet the writer himself praised the purges in which his colleagues were killed. Others did not laud the executions, yet were careful not to protest nor to show any independence of style and spirit whatsoever. When in post-Stalin days Ilya Ehrenburg was asked for reasons of his survival in the purges, he replied: "Lottery luck." But the truth was that all through the Stalinist era Ehrenburg kept his skepticism and liberalism to himself; that his writings were always one long ode to the dictator. As Khrushchev in politics, so Ehrenburg in literature dared to denounce Stalin's gory deeds only after his death.

3 Émigré Literature: Bunin, Nabokov, and Others

As previously noted, a number of writers who could not accept the Bolshevik revolution left the country and lived and continued to write in the West. It might be worth-while to look briefly at the careers of a few of these.

Ivan Bunin made his home in France, at times in Paris, but mainly at Grasse on the French Riviera. Throughout the 1920s and '30s there was a sizable Russian readership outside the Soviet Union—in the independent Baltic states, Poland, Rumania, but particularly Yugoslavia and other Balkan countries, also in Germany, France, and the United States, and in fact all over the world, wherever Russian émigrés were by then scattered. A number of Russian-language magazines and newspapers, also book publishing houses, some quite prosperous, were active among such colonies. Bunin's works graced the top of the list sought to be published and read.

In fact, at times, even if precariously, many such émigré books found their way across the border into the Soviet Union, to its eager readers. As shown in Jacques Deval's 1934 French comedy, *Tovaritch*, the Russians could still take pride in their own; in that play, Russian émigrés working as servants in Paris give to a Soviet official, who once tortured them, the jewels they have taken with them—for they finally agree that the return of these jewels will help "Mother Russia." So were Bunin and other émigré writers as willing to find a Soviet readership as those readers in the homeland were ready to get hold of those émigré books, those jewels of plot and style, whenever these made their way to them.

Bunin's writings in his Western exile were full of nostalgia for the home country and the old days. His *Mitina lyubov'* (1924–25; *Mitya's Love*) is a short novel of adolescence and the battle between flesh and spirit; Mitya in his torment kills himself. The setting, a nobleman's estate, is alluringly projected. *Zhizn' Arsenyeva; istoki dnei* (1927, *Life of Arsenyev*; in English, 1930, *The Well of Days*) began a long work of autobiographical fiction, full of scenes of provincial life in the tradition of the best of the nineteenth-century Russian classics but in a brilliant manner all his own. Bunin also continued to write distinguished short stories, as well as priceless personal reminiscences of Tolstoy and Chekhov. In 1933, amid much acclaim, he became the first Russian-born writer to win the Nobel Prize for literature.

Making his home in France, Bunin yet remained a thorough Russian. Nonetheless, until his death at eighty-three in 1954, Ivan Bunin stubbornly refused to return to Russia despite all the inducements offered by the Communist rulers. Even in 1951, while Stalin was still alive, the *Great Soviet Encyclopedia* made some comments on Bunin which were not altogether unfavorable. Bunin's bitter anti-Soviet feelings notwithstanding, the Soviet government beginning with Khrushchev's time ordered large editions of his fiction and poetry to be published in the Soviet Union with lavish praise. Yet, as Bunin's works are now voluminously reprinted in Russia, this is being done quite selectively—his sharply anti-Soviet writings are carefully omitted. Today the Soviet reader high and low considers Bunin very much his own writer, a classic writer on the plane of Alexander Pushkin, Ivan Turgenev, and Lev Tolstoy, and not the least element in the adulation is the profound beauty of Bunin's old-Russian style.

The expatriate career of Dmitry Merezhkovsky was less successful; in any event, his best work was already accomplished long before he went into exile, in which he died in 1941. In 1922 he had attacked the Soviet régime from Paris, in *Tsarstvo Antikhrista* (*The Kingdom of Antichrist*). In their long exile years in the West he and his wife Zinaida Hippius were busy with politics and religious philosophy more than with fiction and poetry. Yet, Merezhkovsky's early historical novels, translated into foreign languages, are still being read while his essays and his wife's Symbolist poetry are largely forgotten.

Mikhail Osorgin (pseudonym of Mikhail Ilyin, 1878–1942), who began his émigré career of two decades in 1922 when he was expelled from Soviet Russia on Lenin's orders, produced in his lifetime a prolific total of twenty-four volumes of novels and short stories as well as hundreds of articles and essays. Both at home and in his Western exile he was liked by his readers for his spiritual youthfulness, a lively optimism ever winning over the undertone of his lyric melancholy, and always a subtle identification with nature. On becoming an émigré he wrote a novel about the first years of the revolution, *Sivtsev ovrazhek* (1928 and, second edition, 1929), which proved the most popular of all his writings. Translated into English as *Quiet Street*, it was a best seller in America in the early 1930s (helped by a Book-of-the-Month selection). His other books of the 1920s and '30s were the novels *Svidetel' istorii* (*An Eyewitness to History*) and *Vol'nyi kamenshchik* (*The Free Mason*), also the short-story collections *Tam gde byl shchastliv* (*Where I Was Happy*), *Proisshestviya zelyonogo mira* (*Happenings of the Green World*), and *Chudo na ozere* (*The Miracle on the Lake*). He lived in Paris most of his twenty years of Western exile, and died in the so-called Vichy zone of France during the war.

Ivan Shmelyov (1875–1950) and Boris Zaitsev (1881–1972) in their long years as émigrés in the West had admiring readers for their gentle fiction and reminiscences about old Moscow and other Central Russian scenes and for their staunch fealty to the Russian Orthodox Church. Translations of their works into foreign languages have been scant. Shmelyov's works tend to be rather more melancholy than those of Zaitsev, possibly because there was more tragedy in the life of the former: in the aftermath of the civil war in the Crimea, Shmelyov's only son was executed by a Communist firing squad.

In this recital of the highlights of the rich literature of Russian émigrés, let us also mention the life and work of George (Gaito) Gazdanov, a writer of Russian-Osetin origin (1903–71). Coming to the West as a youth, he began his writing in Paris and continued it in Munich. He was a taxi driver and so came to know the night world of Paris criminals and prostitutes. During the Second World War he was in the resistance. He preferred French and other Western themes and characters for his novels and short stories even as he wrote in Russian. In English two of his novels are known: *The Specter of Alexander Wolf* (1950) and *Buddha's Return* (1951). One of his best creations, a novelette *Probuzhdeniye* (*Awakening*), a haunting tale of unusual psychological insight, has been published in Russian only.

Among the few other émigré writers who achieved translation into Western languages, Mark Aldanov (Landau, 1886–1957) made a valuable contribution with his historical novels (on Napoleon, Beethoven, Lenin). And Aleksei Remizov's prose, though complicated and quite obscure even in his native tongue, was well translated into French.

Of the prerevolutionary Russian humorists who emigrated West, Arkady Averchenko (1881–1925) and Nadezhda Teffi (1875–1952; real name, Nadezhda Lokhvitskaya) should be singled out. Before the revolution Averchenko was famous as the founder and editor of the St. Petersburg magazine of humor, *Satirikon,* as well as the author of biting satire. After the revolution his funny stories aimed at both the Communists and the émigrés drew the appreciative laughter of Lenin himself. Teffi's longer career gave her a more prolific opportunity of mocking her fellow émigrés good-naturedly. The works of both writers are avidly read both in the USSR and among the émigrés even in these mid-1970s, but very little of either has been translated into Western languages. Both deserve non-Russian readers.

The poetry of such émigrés as Konstantin Balmont, Vyacheslav Ivanov, and Vladislav Khodasevich, although far more understandable than Remizov's prose, also failed to find foreign translators and readers.

Two poets became far better known as literary critics and theorists. Viktor Shklovsky (born in 1893) did not stay an émigré for long but returned to Soviet Russia where, originally a Formalist, he developed his teaching of distorting reality by legitimate and effective literary devices, and proved to be an important influence on such writers as Zamyatin, Kaverin, and Olesha. But Georgy Adamovich (1894–1972), an early associate of Gumilyov's Guild of Poets, on emigrating to Paris in 1922, never returned to the Soviet Union but over the years was recognized as the foremost Russian literary essayist in the West.

Finally, standing quite separately, there is the spectacular career of another expatriate Russian, Vladimir Nabokov (1899–). The son of a famous Russian liberal murdered by Russian émigré monarchists in 1922, Nabokov was graduated from Cambridge University and lived in Berlin and Paris, eking out his existence by tutoring and other such ill-paid work. He wrote for émigré publications under the pseudonym of V. Sirin. His early novels include *Mashen'ka* (1926; in English, 1970, as *Mary*); *Korol', dama, valet* (1928; in English, 1968, as *King, Queen, Knave*); *Zashchita Luzhina* (1930; in English, 1964, as *The Defense,* one of the finest chess-player portraits ever penned); *Kamera obscura* (1933; in English, 1938, as *Laughter in the Dark*); and others. He also wrote a number of short stories and, later, a most sensitive autobiography.

Moving to the United States in 1940 and becoming an American university professor, he increasingly forsook Russian themes and stopped writing in Russian. He wrote, in English, the daring and controversial *Lolita* (1955); *Pale Fire* (1962); and *Ada or Ardor: A Family Chronicle* (1969). He declared himself an American writer (of Russian origin, to be sure), but settled in Switzerland. At home in several languages and cultures, translated widely, his books best-sellers in astronomical figures, Nabokov is indeed an international writer.

He has never returned to Russia, not even for a brief visit. He is derided by the Party and government, by the state-paid critics, as a depraved man and a decadent writer. His books are banned, be they in Russian or English. But they are smuggled in and are being read avidly, mostly by intellectuals, and to a lesser extent by others, too. Older readers highly approve the Russian originals of such early novels as *The Defense* and *Dar* (*The Gift*), but, being puritanical, disapprove of *Lolita* and *Ada* most definitely. Younger readers drink in all of Nabokov. But both categories are repelled by Nabokov's style in his own translation of *Lolita* from its English original into Russian. Mrs. Ellendea Proffer, who on her visits to the Soviet Union talked to many Russians about Nabokov, states: "Even Nabokov's most ardent fans dislike the Russian translation of *Lolita*. It is sad to report, but almost without exception Russians find Nabokov's translation clumsy and even ungrammatical; they express surprise that the author [of earlier unique prose] could write so poorly." In *Lolita*'s translation, they feel, "he has forgotten" his earlier brilliant Russian. The price, we may add, of creating in another language too well!

4 Later Gorky

Meanwhile, in the Soviet Union, that "Kingdom of Antichrist" as Merezhkovsky branded it, the novel had been slowly but steadily growing. Gorky, already deep in revolutionary literature—though in his later days he showed some doubts and did not really make peace with the new régime until 1928—was a pacesetter. Even during the years when he was out of the country (1921–28, when he again spent most of his time in Sorrento), Gorky's influence remained strong. His own various autobiographical volumes, such as *Detstvo* (1913; *My Childhood*), *V lyudiakh* (1915; *In the World*), and *Vospominaniya o Tolstom* (1919; *Reminiscences of Tolstoy*), he followed with one that goes with the first two of these, *Moi universitety* (1923; *My University Days*) and an extra volume, still personal, *Zapiski iz dnevnika* (1924; *Fragments from my Diary*). In the early 1920s, Gorky also published various short stories in Russia, some of the best of them including "Rasskaz o bezotvetnoi lyubvi" ("A Tale of Unrequited Love"), "Mordovka," and "Rasskaz o geroye" ("A Tale of a Hero").

Gorky returned to novel-writing with *Delo Artamonovykh* (1924; *The Artamanovs' Business*), a family-chronicle story of three generations of Russian capitalists. Gorky closed his career as an imaginative writer with an unfinished "epic" novel which ran to four volumes, *Zhizn' Klima Samgina* (1927–36; *Klim Samgin's Life*), whose first volume, *Sorok let* (1927; *Forty Years* or *Bystander*) had a large sale in translation in English-speaking countries. This tetralogy, which offers a crowded canvas of Russian intellectual life for four decades, is formally awkward, diffuse, and frequently dull despite its occasionally fine vignettes. It is characteristic of Gorky's work, not only rambling but also at times badly written, though now and then vigorous in portraiture and description, and of historical value for its picture of the period it covers. (In his later life Gorky also wrote several plays; these will be discussed in relation to the Soviet theater.)

Gorky, although he voluntarily returned in 1928 to live under a government he had sometimes been doubtful of, remained something of a free spirit who referred to himself jestingly as the Pope of Russian literature. Actually, Gorky never wrote anything set in the years after the revolution. (In this he somewhat resembled the German playwright, Bertolt Brecht, who although he chose to live in East Germany after the Second World War, never wrote a play about life under Communism.) Gorky's friends used to say that he was an institution rather than a man, and he frequently helped Soviet writers to get out of trouble when they violated some of the edicts laid down by the Party. Further, he was friendly to liberal-minded groups such as the earlier-mentioned Serapion Brothers; but freedom of expression was hardly compatible with Stalinist authoritarianism and, by 1936, when Gorky died, writers and other artists under the Stalin rule had to stay carefully within the limits of the Party line.

Gorky's death in a Moscow hospital was recalled two years later, in 1938, during a purge trial of Soviet politicians and doctors, when it was officially explained as "a medical murder" by his physicians allegedly obeying the orders of Genrikh Yagoda, one of Stalin's secret-police chiefs. In time it was established, however, that Gorky died of poisoned candy given to him on Stalin's own orders. For Gorky, finally disillusioned with the Soviet régime, had wanted to leave the Soviet Union for Italy. Stalin prevented this departure because he had wished to avoid the international scandal that would have resulted from Gorky's flight. According to some reports, Gorky's manuscripts of his last few years, containing a passionate denunciation of the murderous Stalinist régime, were confiscated by the secret police and remain unpublished to this day, their whereabouts unknown.

5   *Babel, Sholokhov, Leonov*

So far, several of the early Soviet poets have been discussed, as well as the enduring censorship controls over literature. Now, the early fiction of the new state—that is, up to the Second World War—will be reviewed, as well as some of the poets not so far mentioned, and the Soviet dramatists. Later poets, more detailed accounts of the more recent phases of censorship, and present-day fiction writers will all be given in a subsequent section. At present, then, the concern is with early-Soviet fiction writers.

In spite of restrictions, some fine novels were being turned out by Mikhail Sholokhov, Leonid Leonov, and others. But before considering some of these writers who survived—as Sholokhov and Leonov did—it might be interesting to consider the fate of one of the popular early writers of the Soviet régime, Isaac Babel.

Born in Odessa in 1894, Babel was the son of a Jewish merchant; he went in his youth to St. Petersburg and in 1916 his writings appeared in Gorky's magazine, *Letopis'* (*Annals*), with two tales which brought on prosecution for pornography. Gorky stood by him but, believing that the next stories Babel submitted to the magazine were not up to his best work, rejected them, causing Babel to refrain from further attempts to publish until the early 1920s. Then he reappeared with a number of short stories, many of them incorporated in *Odesskiye rasskazy* (1923–24; *Odessa Tales*) and in *Konarmiya* (1926; *Red Cavalry*).

The fiction in the latter volume was based largely on Babel's experiences as a member of Commander Semyon Budyonny's army in the Soviet republic's war against Poland. Written in the tradition of *skaz* (vivid colloquialism), Babel's tales were full of violent incident with some psychological probing; the stories of the Red cavalry tell graphically of the pillaging, raping, and killing of war. The tales were at once greeted warmly in the Soviet Union—and widely read in translation in the world outside—but later they were sternly criticized in Russia. Budyonny had at first hailed the stories, but later found them destructive. Babel was again in trouble.

He continued to write, however; his *Yevreiskiye rasskazy* (1927; *Jewish Tales*) contained further Odessa stories. Sometime after his article on Maxim Gorky in 1938, Babel sank into silence, or out of life; there is no clear account of what happened to him. Various sources, including his widow living in Paris and his daughter in New York, have revealed that Babel was arrested near Moscow on May 15, 1939; was sentenced either to death or prison by a military court on January 26, 1940; and died in a concentration camp on March 17, 1941. There are, however, other accounts of his disappearance, most of them connected with forced-labor camps, and one report that he was shot immediately after his trial in 1940. But Babel's talent was eventually remembered behind the Iron Curtain; a posthumous collection of his stories was issued in 1957, and in 1960, his contemporary, Konstantin Paustovsky, published a memoir of him. Ironically, these posthumous tributes came a long time after the man's own sufferings, and as to what those were we can only guess.

Among the Soviet fiction writers who have conformed, the one with the greatest prestige, nationally and internationally, is Mikhail Sholokhov. He has written extensively of the Don region where he was born (1905) and grew up. Young Sholokhov may have briefly been a soldier; he was in any event soon a Bolshevik statistician. His first volume of stories came out in 1925, *Donskiye rasskazy* (*Tales of the Don*), followed by *Lazorevaya step'* (1926; *The Azure Steppe*), both volumes concerned with the Don Cossacks in the civil war and under the first years of Leninist rule.

The first part of Sholokhov's masterwork came out in 1928 and has since appeared in several volumes over the years: *Tikhiy Don* (*The Quiet Don*; in English translation *And Quiet Flows the Don*), which for its scope has been compared (first by Gorky) to Tolstoy's *War and Peace*. Sholokhov wrote in a somewhat different vein in *Podnyataya tselina* (1931–60; *Virgin Soil Upturned*, also translated as *Seeds of Tomorrow*, its final volume as *Harvest on the Don*), this work being celebrated as an example of Socialist realism. Here is a tragicomedy of the collectivization of the Don Cossacks. The Sovietizing of the farmlands is opposed by independent-spirited peasants, meeting opposition from the principal character in the novel, a sailor from Leningrad named

Semyon Davydov, who is an honest chairman of the *kolkhoz* (collective farm). He and other collectivists who come into the Don area to set up these communal farms are killed, but other men whom the author portrays as good arrive to take their places, and the process goes on. The various volumes of the series are full of high poetry and sharp realism, and the rustic types are vigorously and colorfully presented.

It is *The Quiet Don,* however, which across its many sections proves to be Sholokhov's most impressive achievement. It is for one thing less propagandistic than *Virgin Soil Upturned* and *Harvest on the Don,* which in post-Stalinist days have come in for criticism (somewhat matching that of Stalin by Nikita Khrushchev) by a younger Soviet writer, Lyuben Kabo. Sholokhov, as mentioned earlier, has conformed to the Soviet system, and this must be taken into account in reading his books; he was even a member of the board of the Union of Soviet Writers which expelled Boris Pasternak at the time of the *Zhivago* affair. A rumor from Moscow says that Khrushchev himself talked Sholokhov out of having Davydov in *Virgin Soil Upturned* commit suicide in disgust: in the published version of the story, Davydov is killed by a White counterrevolutionary.

Objections of propagandist trends rarely apply to the volume of *The Quiet Don,* whose central figure is Grigory Melekhov, Cossack native of the Don basin, who first fights for Russia in the 1914 war against the Central Powers and then, as an officer in the Red Army, in the civil conflict against the forces representing the former tsar. His life is complicated by his love affair (he is himself married) with Aksinya, the wife of a neighbor. Eventually Grigory joins the counterrevolutionary White Army, although he paradoxically still has faith that the Bolsheviks will eventually establish a good government. In the course of this complicated narrative, Grigory again joins the Red Army, but at last returns to his native village, making his farewell to arms by coming back to his small son.

"Little son. . . . little son. . . ."
Then he took his son by the hand. Gazing greedily with

dry, ecstatically burning eyes into the boy's face he asked:
"How are you all? How's Aunty, Polyushka—are they
alive and well?"

Still not looking at his father, Mishatka quietly answered:

"Aunty Dunya's well, but Polyushka died in the au-
tumn—of diphtheria. And Uncle Mikhail's a soldier. . . ."

And now the thing that Grigory had dreamed during so
many sleepless nights had come to pass. He stood at the
gate of his own home, holding his son by the hands.

This was all life had left to him, all that for a little
longer gave him kinship with the earth and with the spa-
cious world which lay glittering under the chilly sun.

There is a Tolstoyan strain in this ending, as there is in
much of the vast and elaborate action of the book, with its
accounts of family life, of men under arms, of battles, of love
affairs, of conflicting allegiances. Perhaps modern readers
need a Sholokhov to demonstrate how complicated it is to
keep alive and to maintain a point of view during the shifts
and terrors of authoritarian régimes—in any event, few living novelists can equal the intensity and the energy which
Sholokhov concentrates in his dynamic panorama of the
volumes comprising *The Quiet Don*.

Among Soviet Russia's other leading novelists is Leonid
Leonov, born in 1899. Although a native of Moscow, he was
of peasant origin; his father was a minor journalist, and at
the time of the civil war the younger Leonov became a staff
member on a Red newspaper, later fighting in the war itself.
Leonov began writing poems and sketches in 1915–18 and
short stories in the early 1920s, among the latter "Derevyan-
naya koroleva" ("The Wooden Queen"), "Bubnovyi valet"
("Knave of Diamonds") and "Gibel' Yegorushki" ("Yego-
rushka's End"), tales which mixed shrewdly realistic observation with Gogol-like fantasy.

For a time after the war, Leonov lived up in Arkhangelsk,
where his father had once been exiled by the tsar. Leonov's
first novel, *Barsuki* (1924; *The Badgers*), is the story of be-
whiskered Moscow merchants of the last days of the tsar, and

of two brothers, Semyon and Pashka, brought into the city from a village to learn the ways of business. Pashka becomes a Communist, but Semyon, who loves the soil, returns to his native village and, as "Comrade Anton," leads a rebellion there against Bolshevik rule; he and his fellow peasants who hide out in the woods are the badgers of the story, ultimately defeated. Leonov wrote his novel with admirable detachment; the book brought praise from Gorky, who told him that he did not find in its three hundred pages any trace of "that maudlin, prettifying manner that has been long the rule in Russian writings about the peasantry."

Leonov's next novel, Vor (1927; The Thief), was set in the time of the New Economic Policy and showed the influence of Dostoyevsky. The protagonist's very name, Dmitry (Mit'ka), is Dostoyevskian, and so to some extent is the backward look of the novel, emblematic of the period when the revolution was slowing down and becoming more aware that it existed upon the ruins of the old order. Mit'ka Vekshin had believed in the revolution and had served with distinction in the civil war, but he feels that killing men in battle is one thing and that twisting their bodies in a torture chamber is quite another; so he refuses to work for the secret police. Instead he becomes the thief, an underworld leader, echoing Dostoyevsky's Raskolnikov in believing that his crimes are justifiable; and, like Raskolnikov, he at the end turns toward possible regeneration, in this case through a truly Leonovist solution, by turning to the soil.

As a story, The Thief is often diffuse and melodramatic. One of its technical features is its novel-within-a-novel, somewhat resembling André Gide's The Counterfeiters in that one of the characters is writing a story about all the people in the book. Politically, The Thief seems negative, or even neutral; and the world outside Russia generally regards it as Leonov's finest novel. It didn't appear in a recent collected edition of his works, but the author has subsequently published a revised version of it.

In the middle 1920s, when Leonov wrote The Thief, he was one of the young Russian writers who felt his conscience pinched by the revolution. Was it really a good thing—was it betraying the true principles of Socialism? He had the friendship and protection of Gorky, and he became no more than a *poputchik*, or fellow traveler. Still pursuing his doubts, he wrote two novels about the First Five-Year Plan, *Sot'* (1930; known in English as *Soviet River*) and *Skutarevsky* (1932), in both of which he depicted once again the conflicts between the old life and the new, between the village and the city.

In *Sot'*, Leonov takes for his hero not an outlaw but a conformist, though he shows a certain amount of sympathy to Vissarion, the former White officer who has become a monk; he is the opponent of the hero, a Communist organizer named Uvadyev. The setting is the far northern forest, which Leonov projects dynamically. There, Uvadyev attempts to build a paper mill against the opposition of the local peasants and Vissarion's monks. Uvadyev is a dedicated Communist who regards Peter the Great as just a craftsman, pitiably ignorant of the Marxist approach. Uvadyev and his fellow Communists are victorious and build their paper mill, and Vissarion is murdered. Some of his ideas, such as the coming of a new Attila (evocative of Blok's poem "The Scythians"), are forcefully presented.

In *Skutarevsky*, Leonov showed signs of approaching more closely to Party slogans. The title-character is an aging professor, a noted scientist, who in his association with factory workers and his love for a young Communist girl, finds a new path in life. The book contains a great deal of material about the Soviet rural-electrification system, and about the problems of sabotage—it is one of the ironies of the story that Professor Skutarevsky, after becoming converted to the new life of Socialism, discovers that his son is a saboteur. The tale sounds oversimple, but Leonov's ability to show people in action, and the way he can bring to life the technical achievements of his electrical engineers, combine to make the narrative an interesting one, though somewhat weighted down by the author's increasing tendency to propagandize in his efforts to show how Socialism successfully wins over the intelligentsia.

Leonov's own integration into the Party is indicated in

Doroga na okean (1936; *Road to the Ocean*), whose hero, Kurilov, is a political commissar plotted against by a former White-army officer named Gleb. It is a story full of complex human relationships, including Kurilov's love affairs. And, despite his belief in the Party, Kurilov refuses to expose his brother-in-law, Omelichev, whom he discovers to be a counterrevolutionary. Omelichev works on the railway which plays an important part in the book; Leonov even investigates the railway's historical past. The author himself comes into the story as a character, discussing with Kurilov the perfect world of the Socialist future—the ocean of the title—and the triumph, in war, of the Soviets over all other nations.

Leonov's career goes on, and in 1953 he wrote *Russkiy les* (*Russian Forest*), a somewhat more objective novel which protests against the depletion of the country's resources—the word *les* in the title, which means both forest and scaffolding, signifies not only those natural resources but also the country's ability to recover from the ravages of war.

A writer of no great original vision, one who at last came to welcome Party guidance, Leonov nevertheless writes at times magnetically about the subjects previously mentioned, the reforestation program, the management of railways, the electrification achievements—when he is not being overly tendentious he is an extremely interesting author, and certainly one of Russia's earliest heralds of ecology. He is also a dramatist, whose plays will be mentioned in the discussion of the Soviet theater.

6 Some Other Novelists

Two of the prerevolutionary Russian novelists, Alexander Kuprin and Aleksei Tolstoy, have been mentioned earlier as having left the country after the establishment of the Bolshevik government and as having subsequently returned. Kuprin's early books, *The Duel*, published in 1905, and *Yama: The Pit*, published in 1912, have already been discussed. During his residence in Paris, Kuprin wrote several volumes of fiction, including *Yunkera* (1933; *The Junkers*), another of his stories of prerevolutionary army life. In 1937, sick and old, Kuprin returned to his homeland amid great acclamation, and the next year he died there.

Aleksei Tolstoy, who had inherited the title of count, underwent training as an engineer. A rather moderate Social Democrat in 1905, he became a correspondent in the First World War and, after it, served with the Whites. He stayed in Paris until 1923 and then returned to Russia to become a distinguished Soviet author.

His career as a writer had begun earlier, with stories and poems, the most important of the latter collected in *Lirika* (1907; *Lyrics*) and *Za sinimi rekami* (1909; *Beyond Blue Rivers*). *Detstvo Nikity* (1920; *Nikita's Childhood*) was written in Tolstoy's time of expatriation, during which period he also began his most important work, *Khozhdeniye po mukam* (*The Road to Calvary*), completed in 1941. This is a panoramic novel of Russian life before the revolution and during it and the civil war; Tolstoy later rewrote the first section, which originally manifested an anti-Soviet stand. In 1937, Aleksei Tolstoy's *Khleb* (*Bread*) provided a spirited narrative of the defense, at the time of the revolution, of Tsaritsyn (later Stalingrad). The novel glorifies Stalin at the expense of Trotsky.

When Tolstoy died in 1945 he had not completed his famous historical novel, *Pyotr Pervyi* (1929–45; *Peter the First*), a portrait not only of the man who created modern Russia, but of the nation at that time. Peter is shown as often clumsy and awkward, as Russia itself was then, but also as driving himself on to modernize his country. Tolstoy introduces Peter's fiercely attractive mistress, Anna Mons; Eudoxia, the wife he didn't love; and at last the peasant girl who was to become empress as Catherine I. The tsar's battles at court, with the recalcitrant boyars, as well as the military campaigns against the brilliant Charles XII of Sweden, are all vividly depicted, but the story is often spoiled by the Soviet tendency to indulge in hero-worship of Peter the Great.

A far more honest author who wrote historical novels was

Yuri Tynyanov (1894–1943), a scholar and translator, whose *Kukhlya* (1925) was a fictional study of the poet Wilhelm Küchelbecker, a Decembrist conspirator and friend of Pushkin. In *Smert' Vazir-Mukhtara* (1927–28; *Death and Diplomacy in Persia*), Tynyanov dealt with events surrounding the assassination of the playwright Alexander Griboyedov in Teheran in 1829. Tynyanov kept to the period with his *Pushkin* (1936–43), a circumstantial and full-bodied but unfinished biographical novel about the poet. The artistic and philosophic significance of this novelist's work was brought out in post-Stalinist times by the nonconformist Soviet critic Arkady Belinkov (who later defected to the West) in his justly celebrated book on Tynyanov.

A fearless nonconformist in both eras, tsarist and Soviet, Yevgeny Zamyatin (1884–1937) had been exiled before the revolution nor would he later accept the Communist régime. In tsarist times he had studied shipbuilding and became an engineer while engaged in underground radical activities as a Bolshevik member of the Social Democrats. The tsar's secret police sent him away from St. Petersburg to live in a sparsely populated district in Lakhta, where he wrote provincial tales. At the time of the First World War, Zamyatin was assigned to go to England as an engineer, to construct icebreakers. He subsequently satirized English life in such stories as "Ostrovityane" (1922; "The Islanders"). An important influence on younger writers in postrevolutionary Russia, Zamyatin was one of the earlier-mentioned Serapion Brothers' literary group. Most of his writing took the form of short stories; his method was a realism so intensified that it almost becomes surrealism; because of its abrupt angles and use of simultaneity it has been designated as Cubist.

Zamyatin's most ambitious work was his novel *My* (*We*), apparently completed in 1920 and first published, though not in its complete form, in a Russian-language magazine in Prague in 1924 (translated from Czech back into Russian); subsequent versions came out in English and French, though the book was blocked in the Soviet Union. The uproar over its appearance in other countries was comparable to the later uproar over Pasternak's *Doctor Zhivago*, for Zamyatin's *We* was regarded as not exactly praising the Soviet system. It is a utopian novel set in a socialized society in the twenty-sixth century, and the characters have numbers rather than names. The book probably influenced Aldous Huxley in the writing of *Brave New World* and George Orwell in the composition of *1984*. Zamyatin, in an autobiographical sketch in 1925, said he had been a Bolshevik before the revolution but was not one at that time. Violently attacked by his fellow authors in the Soviet Union, he resigned in 1929 from the Writers' Union. Two years later—it is suspected with Gorky's help—he was permitted to leave the country.

In June 1931, in his bold petition to Stalin, as Zamyatin requested permission to leave the Soviet Union for good, he argued that being forced to live in the USSR with no freedom to write was "tantamount to a death sentence," and that "in the Soviet code of laws the next lower punishment after a death sentence is the criminal's expulsion from his country." Stalin apparently agreed with this argument. Miraculously, he let Zamyatin emigrate to Western Europe. It is of interest to note that in the West, in the last six years of his life, Zamyatin had little to do with other Russian émigrés, clearly not classing himself with them. Before his death in France in 1937, he brought out the first part of *Bich bozhiy* (*The Scourge of God*), a novel about Attila the Hun which contained overtones of criticism of the Russian revolution.

In that year of 1929 when Zamyatin resigned from the Writers' Union, another author, Boris Pilnyak (pen name of Boris Vogau, of Volga-German origin, 1894–1938 or 1939), was expelled from it, at a time when he was its president. Pilnyak, who had been graduated from the Moscow Commercial Institute (later the Plekhanov Institute) in his twenty-sixth year, in 1920, was in his youthful writings admittedly the disciple of the earlier Aleksei Remizov, who was also an influence upon Zamyatin. Remizov, himself in the line of Gogol, dealt often in the technique of the *skaz*, mentioned earlier as the tale embodying idiomatic extravagances. Significantly (as already noted), this mentor of Pilnyak's left Russia in the early 1920s to settle, like various other émigrés, in Paris.

Pilnyak's first fame was the result of his series of sketches which have the effect of a novel, *Golyi god* (1920; *The Naked Year*), hailed as the first large-scale fictional account of the aftereffects of the revolution. The writer of a vigorous, ornamental, chromatic prose, Pilnyak became a highly popular author in Russia. But he was not always appreciated by the critics, who—as everyone knows—function in the Soviet Union on a somewhat official basis. His most severe trouble came, like Zamyatin's and, subsequently, Pasternak's and Solzhenitsyn's, from publishing a book outside the country. Pilnyak's short novel, *Krasnoye derevo* (1929; *Mahogany*) came out in a Russian language edition in Germany, and this created a brouhaha in Moscow. The irony of the situation lies in the fact that the Berlin appearance of the story didn't have the author's sanction. In *Mahogany*, the two central characters are a young Trotskyite engineer and his uncle who believes in a kind of Christianized, charitable Communism.

The story itself never appeared in the Soviet Union, though Pilnyak put parts of it, with changed emphasis, into his novel *Volga vpadayet v Kaspiyskoye more* (1930; *The Volga Falls into the Caspian Sea*). This is a Five-Year-Plan story about a purely imaginary hydroelectric project, the construction of a dam near Moscow, whose river is to be made navigable for larger ships by the diversion of the Volga. Like Gladkov's *Energy*, that novel about the actual Dnieper Dam, *The Volga Falls* is overburdened with technical detail. Pilnyak in this book seemed to be suggesting that enterprises of the new state were costly in terms of human lives, here specifically the character Ivan Ozhogov (one of the people in *Mahogany*), who is drowned at the opening of the new dam. And several of the engineers in the novel, in a kind of protest against enslavement by the state, choose to die.

Pilnyak had uttered strenuous public recantations after *Mahogany*, but *The Volga Falls* didn't silence his official critics. He made several attempts to redeem himself, including *Okey* (1932), a piece of impressionist fiction attacking life in America. But nothing helped; Pilnyak was arrested in the late 1930s; like Babel he died in imprisonment, shot either in 1938 or 1939 (the exact date remains unknown) on charges of being "a Japanese spy." He had indeed once visited Japan, and written about it quite innocently.

The main reason for Pilnyak's doom was the political courage he had displayed in 1926 when he published a magazine story in which, in a thinly disguised form, he described how in October 1925 Stalin had caused Commander Mikhail Frunze's death by ordering him to undergo a wholly unnecessary surgical operation which ended fatally. (Stalin wanted Frunze's high post of war commissar for his friend Kliment Voroshilov.)

Of the early nonconformists who managed to survive despite the heavy guns of Party criticism aimed at them, Yuri Olesha (1899–1960) was as original as he proved to be controversial. His work as a playwright will be discussed later, but here we must single out his brilliant novel *Zavist'* (1927; *Envy*), which was widely acclaimed before the official critics realized in dismay that it was an ironic celebration of the individual as opposed to the state. Similarly individualistic, although writing in a less tense and colorful style, Panteleimon Romanov (1884–1938) aroused much interest and discussion with such novels as *Bez cheremukhi* (1926; *Without Cherry Blossoms*), about the cynical approach by the new Soviet youth to love as something simply biological and not at all romantic, of which attitude the author disapproved, and the lengthy *Rossiya* (1926–36; *Russia*), which praised old spiritual values as against strict Communist dogma.

A literary figure of great stature and true worth, Konstantin Paustovsky (1892–1968) was born in Moscow but his ancestral roots were in the South and West: on the paternal side he was descended from land-tilling Cossacks of the Ukraine, while his mother came from an impoverished, noble Polish family. In 1914–15 he was a medical orderly in the First World War, and later worked as a trolley motorman and ticket seller in Moscow, a factory worker and fisherman in the South, and back in Moscow as a teacher of Russian literature. He began writing as a journalist in 1917, served in the Red Army during the civil war, and returned to newspaper work afterward. His novels, novelettes, and short stories began to appear in the 1920s. Of his writings, Vstre-chnyie korabli (1928; Ships That Pass) and Kara-Bugaz (1932) were notable, but his widest readership came with his autobiographical Povest' o zhizni (A Story of Life), embracing the first two volumes Dalyokiye gody (Distant Years) and Bespokoinaya yunost' (Stormy Youth), both appearing in 1956, and Nachalo nevedomogo veka (The Beginning of an Unknown Age) as its third volume in 1958. Although on occasion Paustovsky had to pay lip service to the Soviet régime, he avoided servility and dishonesty as much as the Stalinist years allowed such rare freedom. For his humanity no less than for his limpid style he gained a wide popularity, particularly in the freer 1950s and '60s. He was amply translated into many foreign languages.

A writer who stands uniquely separate from the general stream and substance of twentieth-century Russian literature, Alexander Grin (Grinevsky) was born in 1880 in utter poverty in Vyatka, Northeastern Russia; he died in 1932 in a yet worse destitution in the Crimea. The son of an exiled Pole, said to be a cousin of Joseph Conrad (né Korzeniow-ski), Grin grew up to be a hobo, a sailor, a low-paid day laborer of many kinds, a tsarist army soldier and deserter, an underground revolutionary, and a political prisoner. He began to write in his youth, and his first book came out in 1908. Quite early in his writings, he would escape the Russian reality of his day, creating stories of complete fantasy. In time he constructed what his admirers called "Grinlandia" —a totally imagined land of semitropical ports and adventurers of Scandinavian- and British-sounding names.

In 1917 he welcomed the first revolution that overthrew the monarchy (March), but not the second wherein Lenin's Bolsheviks seized power (November). During the civil war he was drafted into the Red Army, and nearly perished from typhus and hunger, but Gorky, learning of his plight, saved him.

In his lifetime he wrote six novels and scores of stories. His best-known fantasy, Alyie parusa (The Crimson Sails), was begun in 1920 and completed in late 1922. The collections Gladiatory (1925; The Gladiators) and Ogon' i voda

(1930; *Fire and Water*) are typical of his exotic tales. But the Communist Party and the Soviet government frowned upon his worship of Edgar Allan Poe (he hardly ever parted with a portrait of Poe), his rejection of the Soviet world around him, and his creation of that whimsical, romantic "Grinlandia."

Soviet state publishing houses often refused to publish him; he and his wife continued to starve despite his fame; toward the end of his life, Grin would try, with his bow and arrow, to shoot birds in the Crimean woods—for there was no other food in his ramshackle house. Yet such writers as Olesha, Fadeyev, and Katayev gratefully recognized his mastery and his influence upon them. And, notwithstanding the official Soviet censure, multitudes of readers sought out Grin's escapist tales, since these multitudes also wanted to forget their wretched existence.

Following Stalin's death the strictures upon Grin's work were relaxed, and new editions of his novels and stories were permitted, especially of *The Crimson Sails*, of which several stage and film versions were eventually made, drawing large audiences. One of the best, warmest appraisals of Grin's tragic life and fantastic talent was written by Konstantin Paustovsky in 1964 (as an introduction to Grin's *Novelly-Alyie parusa*, reprinted by the *Moskovskyi rabochyi* publishing house).

But there also was, through the Soviet decades, ever since their beginning, a body of literature where praise of the Communists and their régime was sung with various degrees of sincerity and talent. One of the best of the early post-revolutionary novels was Konstantin Fedin's *Goroda i gody* (1924; *Cities and Years*), which like Aleksei Tolstoy's *The Road to Calvary* deals on a large scale with pre-1914, revolutionary and civil-war Russia. Fedin, who had served as a journalist on various Red Army papers, was one of the Serapion Brothers' literary group which, it will be remembered, attempted to establish a free and boldly imaginative school of fiction writing in the early 1920s.

The cities in Fedin's novels are Berlin and Moscow. As Fedin himself had been, his protagonist Andrei Startsov is interned in Germany during the First World War. Before the outbreak of hostilities, Andrei meets a young German whom Fedin portrays as of stauncher character than Andrei: Kurt Wahn, who is captured while fighting in Russia during the war. Kurt becomes an ardent Bolshevik, again associated with Andrei after the latter returns to his homeland. Andrei, the vacillating intellectual, is a weak cog in the revolutionary machine, and eventually Kurt shoots him—and the committee sitting in judgment upon him for this act clears him. After the novel was published, Fedin was widely suspected of being on the side of his rather feeble hero.

Technically, *Cities and Years* is rather cinematic, with many jumps backward and forward in time, a method which Fedin also used in his next novel, *Bratya* (1928; *Brothers*). Here his sympathies seem definitely on the side of the artist-intellectual who finds conformity to Soviet life difficult. In this case the hero is a composer named Nikita Karev. He cannot express the revolution adequately in his music, and he also fails in love. The book is less interesting than the controversy it aroused, for a number of Soviet critics accused Fedin of sympathizing with Karev's inability to adjust to the new state. Two years earlier, Fedin's novella *Transvaal* (1926) had also aroused critical antagonism: with this portrait of Swaaker, a farmer of Boer origin who becomes an important figure in the Russian village he has come to, Fedin was accused of being partial to the *kulaks* (well-to-do peasants eventually destroyed by the Soviets).

Fedin's conversion to Soviet ideology was marked by his two-volume work, *Pokhishcheniye Yevropy* (1932–35; *The Rape of Europe*), in which the Western nations of the continent are portrayed as decadent in contrast with the Soviet Union and its effective leadership. The novel is diffuse and often flat, and its second volume, purporting to show the progressive élan of the Soviet Union, is hardly convincing. Trade relations between Russia and other nations play an important part in the story, particularly as they concern a family of Dutch timber merchants who eventually prove themselves to be ineffectual when compared with the vigorous Soviet commissars with whom they deal. Several love stories which cross the borders of Russia add some interest to the novel, but its total effect is rather spiritless. Fedin, however, became one of the most admired authors in Russia, although he had some trouble over his memoirs in 1943; the subsequent phases of his career will be noted later.

Fyodor Gladkov (1883–1958) is a novelist of Volga peasant stock known particularly for his *Tsement* (*Cement*), first serialized in the already mentioned review, *Red Virgin Soil*, in 1925 and published as a book in the following year. It is regarded as an outstanding example of proletarian realism. Gladkov, in his youth exiled to Siberia, felt a kinship with that earlier exile, Dostoyevsky, whose work was an influence on his own, along with that of Andreyev and Gorky. Gladkov first obtained recognition with his short novel *Izgoi* (1912; *The Outcasts*), a severely realistic account of the lives of political prisoners, of whom he wrote again in *Staraya sekretnaya* (1927; *The Old Dungeon*). Gladkov's first serious postrevolutionary attempt at a novel was *Ognennyi kon'* (1923; *The Fiery Steed*), a huge and melodramatic story of the civil war.

As noted earlier, it was *Cement*, in 1925, which brought Gladkov his greatest fame. A pioneer novel about Soviet industrialization, it has for its hero the cement worker Gleb, who is unable to maintain a satisfactory relationship with his wife Dasha. But he does succeed in getting a cement plant reopened. And even if the relationship of Gleb and Dasha rarely gets beyond artificiality, the problems of the factory and the experiences of its workers come through with vivid fidelity. Gladkov attempted further treatment of proletarian problems in *Energiya* (1930–36; *Energy*), concerned with the men who built the Dnieper Dam (completed in 1932); but these men are buried under the weight of technical details of construction. Gladkov placed more emphasis on the human side in *Novaya zemlya* (1931; *The New Land*) and *Tragediya Lyubashi* (1935; *Lyubasha's Tragedy*), which illustrate some of the difficulties of living in a totalitarian society. *Malen'kaya trilogiya* (1936; *A Little Trilogy*) is made up of three sketches satirizing an arriviste, a hypocrite, and a pompous chatterer, as observed by the director of a factory.

An early Soviet historical novel of some note, Aleksei

Chapygin's three-volume *Razin Stepan* (1926–27; *Stepan Razin*), is a vigorous portrait of a seventeenth-century folk hero, viewed of course in terms of Soviet ideology. Chapygin was already a veteran author (born in 1870, he was to die in 1937) who had begun his career in tsarist times. His sketches about the St. Petersburg poor, *Nelyudimyie* (*The Misanthropes*), came out in 1912; three years later, with *Bely skit* (1915; *Snow-Covered Retreat*), Chapygin won the praise of Gorky for these stories of the peasants and their mystic beliefs. The success of *Stepan Razin* in the 1920s was followed by another novel of the same historical period, *Gulyashchiye lyudi* (1935–37; *Roving People*), an account of the seventeenth-century peasant uprisings.

Dying ten years before the purges and thus never given an opportunity either to fall as a victim or ride high as a conformist, the young and gifted Dmitry Furmanov (1891–1926) wrote of his own involvement in the civil war. To him it was recent and glorious history, and this is the overwhelming sense of his novel *Chapayev* (1923), which told of the adventurous guerrilla leader of that name. In 1935 *Chapayev* was made into a vigorous and successful Soviet film.

An author vastly overrated by Soviet officialdom, Nikolai Ostrovsky (1904–36), was a worker's son from the Volyn Province, Southwestern Russia, who out of his experience as a volunteer soldier in the civil war wrote the novel *Kak zakalyalas' stal'* (*How the Steel Was Tempered*; published in English as *The Making of a Hero*, 1932–34). A Communist Party member since 1924, he was much publicized by Stalin's régime as a sterling son of the Soviet system, and considerable sympathy was shown for him when, still a young man, he was overcome by blindness and paralysis, dying at thirty-two. His fiction was used extensively for the Soviet stage and screen.

Among the lesser yet "approved" writers of the 1920s and '30s Alexander Serafimovich (1863–1949; real name Popov) was prolific and often tedious. A Don Cossack by origin, a revolutionary before 1917, he began his writing in northern exile, his first novel *Gorod v stepi* (*The City in the Steppe*) appearing in 1912. Gorky valued and encouraged him. His renown reached its peak in Soviet times with his novel *Zhe-leznyi potok* (1924; *The Iron Torrent*), which romanticized Yepifan Kovtyukh, a historical personage (whom the writer named Kozhukh), a Red Army commander in the civil war times, with the Northern Caucasus as the locale. In the 1930s Serafimovich labored on a large novel *Bor'ba* (*The Struggle*), excerpts from which were published but which remained unfinished. In 1943 he was awarded the Stalin Prize.

Another such safe conformist, Yuri Gherman (born in 1910 in Riga on the Baltic shore) was not without a modicum of talent. His obedient themes were reeducation of man, also patriotic Communist treatments of Russian history, and the ideals of "Socialist morality." His novels include *Rafael iz parikmakherskoi* (1931; *Raphael from the Barbershop*); *Nashi znakomyie* (1934–36; *Our Acquaintances*); and *Bednyi Genrikh* (1934; *Poor Heinrich*); also novelettes *Aleksei Zhmakin* (1937–38) and *Studyonnoye more* (1943; *Ice-Cold Sea*), as well as a number of plays, film-scripts, and short stories. The era of Peter the Great was his subject in the novel *Rossiya molodaya* (1952; *Young Russia*). In 1938–57 Yuri Gherman eulogized the notorious Soviet executioner Feliks Dzerzhinsky, *Rasskazy o Dzerzhinskom* (*Tales about Dzerzhinski*). In 1958 Gherman officially joined the Communist Party.

But conformity, whether sincere or slavish, was never a guaranty of being spared the punishing Stalinist hand in the purges. The case of Yuri Libedinsky (1898–1959) is illustrative. Born in Odessa, but growing up in the Urals, he was an early revolutionary, mainly under the influence of the sweetheart of his childhood and youth, Marianna Gerasimova, the daughter of an underground radical who spent most of his time in tsarist jails or exiles. The girl was being brought up in the home of an uncle, a prosperous miller. The young lovers dreamt of the revolution to come. When it finally came, both joined it, Yuri as a Red warrior, Marianna as a secret policewoman. Enrolling in the Communist Party formally in 1920, Libedinsky made his literary debut with the novel *Nedelya* (1922; *A Week*), which centered around the quelling of a White rebellion. A reviewer in the Moscow *Pravda* hailed it as "the first swallow of Soviet literature." Among Libedinsky's later works the novel *Komissary* (1924–25; *The Commissars*) was notable for its ecstatic praise of Soviet leaders.

He and Marianna were married, and the young beautiful woman continued in her secret police work of apprehending and annihilating the Red Kremlin's enemies, real or imaginary. Suddenly, in the mid-1930s Libedinsky himself was declared such an enemy. Although one of the leaders of RAPP, the Russian Association of Proletarian Writers, he fell in disgrace when the whole organization was disbanded. In 1936 he was expelled from the Union of Soviet Writers, and in 1937 from the Communist Party.

Of course he lost his wife, who soon married another man. In 1937 in a stern letter she lectured him that he "must bravely admit his mistakes" and submit to his "deserved" fate. But soon thereafter, while most unaccountably Libedinsky was restored to his Party membership, Marianna not only was dismissed from her secret police duties, but was even arrested. In the winter of 1939 Libedinsky together with Marianna's new husband waited for many freezing hours and days in front of the infamous Butyrki Prison in Moscow, to be allowed to hand over to the guards some warm clothing, which she would surely need before being sent to a concentration camp.

He dared to write a plea to Stalin on behalf of Marianna, pointing out that she now suffered from an illness of the brain (most likely the result of her cruel secret police work). His letter was never answered. But two years later, in November 1941, hopelessly ill, Marianna was freed and allowed to return to Moscow, to the lodgings of her sister Valeriya, a minor writer, where Libedinsky and his new wife Lidiya visited her. On December 4 of that year, as the Nazi troops were driving toward Moscow, Marianna committed suicide by hanging herself over a toilet seat. Lidiya later reminisced that Libedinsky, crushed, exclaimed to himself: "Your first love hanged herself in a privy, do you understand! Who is responsible? Who?"

Among other writers of the new Soviet era several women

should be named. Olga Forsh (1875–1961), of noble origin, the daughter of the military governor of Central Daghestan, educated in an elite school for girls, she wrote and published stories about Russia's rural life before the revolution (1908–9), and in Soviet times tried to escape official directives by writing about occultism (1920), but later changed to "safe" Soviet themes. Her numerous novels included *Sumasshedshiy korabl'* (1934; *The Crazy Ship*); *Mikhailovskiy zamok* (1946; *The Michael Castle*); and *Perventsy svobody* (1953; *The First-Born of Freedom*).

Marietta Shaginyan (1888–) wrote poems and novels about industrialization of her native Armenia, also about Lenin's family, as well as mystery tales. One of her stories is purported to be by an American worker in Soviet Russia.

Lidiya Seifulina (1899–1954), born in the Southeastern steppes of Orenburg, was the daughter of a Christianized Tatar who became a Russian Orthodox priest and of a Russian peasant woman. She was a teacher and a librarian before she began to write in 1921. Her subjects were the civil war, the new Soviet woman, and life in the provinces. Her greatest popularity was reached in 1926–27, but official critics often attacked her for portraying the negative reality of the Soviet times rather more than stressing the required radiance of the new régime.

Vera Inber (1890–1972) became known in the 1920s as a member of the Constructivist group that believed in including scientific and technological terms and ideas in their writing. Inber displayed considerable narrative force in her book *Synu, kotorogo net* (1927; *To the Non-Existent Son*).

Honest realism as well as calculated sentiment were the ingredients in the writings of Vera Panova (1905–73). She began as a newspaperwoman in her native Rostov-on-the-Don, and during the Second World War was a correspondent on military-hospital trains. In time she wrote a novel about one such train. One of her earliest works was a play— *Ilya Kosogor* (1939), which was followed by two more plays: *Metelitsa* (1941; *The Snowstorm*) and *Provody belykh nochei* (1960; *Farewell to White Nights*). Of her novels and novelettes best-known were *Sputniki* (1946; *Road Compan-*

ions) and *Seryozha* (1955; *Little Serge*). The last-named was made into a popular film, which eventually proved successful also in the United States. At certain times Stalinist critics chided her for her "lack of objectivity" and "digression from Socialist realism."

7   Some Satirists: Ehrenburg, Ilf and Petrov, Zoshchenko

Ilya Ehrenburg (1891–1967), who began as mainly a writer of satire but later changed to a serious vein, was in his time among the best-known Russian authors. We have already noted that, as a young poet, he had left the country after the revolution and the civil war, but eventually returned.

Ehrenburg, born of a middle-class Jewish family in 1891, took part in the 1905 uprising and a few years later was imprisoned; subsequently he traveled through Europe, settling in Paris, where he was influenced by Paul Claudel, Francis Jammes, and other Catholic writers; at one time he even considered becoming a Benedictine monk. On his return to Paris from Russia in 1921, the French police encouraged him over the border, and for a while he lived in Belgium, where he wrote the novel *Neobychainyie pokhozhdeniya Julio Jurenito* (1922; *The Extraordinary Adventures of Julio Jurenito*), first published in Berlin. This is a cynical satire on various nations as supposedly seen by a picaresque Mexican hero.

Ehrenburg wrote many other novels in the 1920s and 1930s—before reaching the pinnacle of his prewar fame in 1940 with *Padeniye Parizha* (1941–42; *The Fall of Paris*) — one of the most renowned of his earlier books being *Lyubov' Zhanny Ney* (1924; *The Love of Jeanne Ney*). This story of a bourgeois French girl and her Russian Communist lover, Andreas, was in 1927 made by G. W. Pabst into a highly successful UFA film which, because of changes in the plot, aroused Ehrenburg's protests. He had earlier written a bitter satire, *Trest D. E.* (1923; *Trust D. E.*), on the possibility of

Europe's being taken over in 1940 by capitalist America. V *Protochnom pereulke* (1927; *A Street in Moscow*) deals with slum life in the Russian capital. In V*toroi den'* (1933; *The Second Day*, also called *Out of Chaos*), Ehrenburg treats the theme of the individual against the mass in a story set amid the construction activities in a steel plant in Siberia; this is one of his finest and most mature novels. Ehrenburg was a war correspondent in the Spanish civil conflict of 1936–39 and in the Second World War; his lively dispatches from battlefronts, now filled with anger as well as satire, were read all over the world.

Ilya Ilf (1897–1937) and Yevgeny Petrov (1903–42) were a team of collaborators on satiric books, notably *Zolotoi telyonok* (1931; *The Little Golden Calf*, in a more recent translation *The Golden Calf*). The pair met in 1925 while fellow reporters in Moscow on the railway workers' newspaper, *Gudok* [The whistle]. Both wrote under pseudonyms; Ilf was born Ilya Fainzilberg. Petrov's actual name was Yevgeny Katayev; his older brother, Valentin Katayev, is himself a satiric novelist, notable above all for *Rastratchiki* (1926; *The Embezzlers*), the amusing story of two clerks in the office of a trust in Moscow who run off with some money and go on a hilarious spree before they are caught and punished. The later books by this elder Kateyev brother, as well as his plays, will be considered subsequently.

Meanwhile, there is his brother Yevgeny who, as Petrov, worked with Ilf on several comic volumes that penetrated beyond Russia to the outer world: the collaboration ended with the death of Ilf, of tuberculosis, in 1937; Petrov, a correspondent at the front in the Second World War, was killed at Sevastopol in 1942. But the popularity of the Ilf and Petrov books has lived on, in other countries as well as in Russia. A new English translation of *The Golden Calf* appeared in 1962.

The first Ilf and Petrov book, suggested by the elder Katayev, was *Dvenadtsat' stulyev* (1928; *Twelve Chairs*, also *Diamonds to Sit On*), the story of "the great manipulator," Ostap Bender, who with several accessories goes on a mad hunt for some diamonds hidden in a chair by its owner in

tsarist times; but although Bender and his cronies can't lo-
cate the money, others do find it and use it for cultural activities sponsored by a Soviet club. "The great manipulator"
is killed at the end, but with all the roguish ability of a character out of *Candide* to resurrect himself, Bender comes back
to life for *The Golden Calf*, the sequel to *Twelve Chairs*.
Here, Bender and three fellow-confidence men, who drive
around in an automobile called the Antelope, chase after a
millionaire who has illegally hoarded his money. But even
when Bender and his friends have taken the money, they
discover that it has no importance in the new state. Through
all this, Ilf and Petrov are Socialist moralists; they disapprove
of Bender even while making him and his adventures extensively funny.

Ilf and Petrov visited the United States during the depression and made a coast-to-coast trip in an automobile, record-
ing their criticisms and pointing up their experiences comically. The resultant book was *Odnoetazhnaya Amerika*
(1936; *One-Storied America*), and for all its satire it was
more amicable than that of many later Soviet travelers. Ilf
and Petrov also wrote about America (Columbus's redis-
covery of it in the twentieth century) in one of the stories
in their collection, *Tonya*. This was published in 1937, the
year of Ilf's death. Two years later, Petrov brought out Ilf's
Zapisnyie knizhki (1939; *Notebooks*), for which he wrote
an interesting preface, providing details of the collaborators'
methods. In the hectic postwar phase of the Stalin régime,
in 1949, the publishing house *Sovetskiy pisatel'* (*The Soviet
Writer*) was scolded in the pages of *Literaturnaya gazeta*
(*Literary gazette*) for reissuing in a single volume those
"ideologically pernicious" Ilf and Petrov novels, *Twelve
Chairs* and *The Golden Calf*.

There were still other writers who added the salt of fun
to Soviet literature, and sometimes, because the committees
who guarded the state were often composed of humorless
men, there was trouble, as in the case of Mikhail Zoshchenko
(1895–1958). He was an irrepressible satirist. He was somewhat in the tradition of Nikolai Gogol, Mikhail Saltykov-
Shchedrin, and other earlier biting writers; his fables carried

a sting because Zoshchenko was a gadfly who took for his targets various social evils in the state which everyone was supposed to admire as perfect.

In the 1920s, after having been a law student at the University of St. Petersburg and alternately a tsarist officer and a member of the Red Army, Zoshchenko became one of the leading figures among the liberally inclined and essentially satirical Serapion Brothers. His early stories, collected as *Rasskazy Nazara Ilyicha gospodina Sinebryukhova* (1922; *The Tales of Nazar Ilyich, Mr. Sinebrukhov*), were concerned with recent and current events such as the war and civil war, as related by a half-educated corporal; as oral tales, they came technically under the definition of the *skaz*. After an attempt at somewhat more objective comic stories, Zoshchenko returned to the form of the *skaz*, adopting as his narrator the average Russian who uses a language midway between the colloquial speech of his class and the rhetoric of Soviet propaganda. One of the country's leading critics, Professor Viktor Vinogradov, attacked Zoshchenko's stories on the ground that he put into the mouths of uneducated people too many literary expressions; Zoshchenko has been defended on the score of that previously mentioned propagandist rhetoric, which in the early years of the Soviet state had a semiliterary flavor and was widely adapted and imitated in everyday discourse.

Some of Zoshchenko's finest work appears in the two volumes of his *Uvazhayemyie grazhdane* (1926 and 1940; *Respected Citizens*), and in the collection *Golubaya kniga* (1934; *The Blue Book*). Over the years it became apparent to Party-line critics that Zoshchenko was not merely a comic writer, but a highly critical one, and he was often castigated for his attitude. His earlier tales seemed comic for their own sake, but as he went on writing, Zoshchenko became the spokesman of disillusionment. Where in earlier stories he had merely poked fun at the difficulties of people in adjusting to new conditions, in his later fiction he seemed to be finding fault with the conditions themselves: housing shortages, profiteering, inefficiency, and other trappings of the bureaucratic state. Even at his bitterest, however, Zoshchenko manifests a sense of the zestfully comic, and his satires are, in the aggregate, the finest to come out of Soviet Russia.

Consider one story, "Kocherga" ("The Poker"), the account of a new government bureau anachronistically set up in an old building heated by six wood-burning stoves for which the ancient caretaker has only one poker. Once when carrying this from one stove to another, he burns one of the office girls, causing the manager to apply for five more pokers. But, as he starts to fill out the requisition for them, the manager can't find the proper plural form of the word *kocherga*; when no one in the bureau can supply it, the old peasant caretaker suggests using the diminutive, so common in peasant speech. The manager, refusing to lower his dignity by descending to commonplace idiom, orders one of his legal assistants to prepare an order for five pokers without directly mentioning them. The legal assistant prepares a draft that is a masterpiece of its kind, but all to no avail; the warehouse reports that there is a shortage of pokers, and in its answer uses the diminutive. Zoshchenko's work is full of such cynical mischief.

In 1933, Zoshchenko expanded his *skaz* technique to novel length in V*ozvrashchonnaya molodost'* (*Youth Restored*), the story of an aging astronomy professor who, after leaving his wife and marrying a flighty young girl, finds that she is deceiving him. The professor suffers a paralytic stroke from which he recovers and then goes back to his first wife, though still yearning for the faithless second one. Soviet critics, who missed the element of the comic implicit in the book, discussed it seriously as a medical treatise; they failed to see that Zoshchenko was also contrasting the drabness of the 1930s with the more exciting epoch of the twenties.

Another novella by Zoshchenko, *Pered voskhodom solntsa* (*Before Sunrise*), began appearing in the magazine *Oktyabr'* (*October*) in 1943 and was suddenly discontinued. *Before Sunrise* is a reminiscential story of childhood and youth, a narrative accused of drawing upon Sigmund Freud, persona non grata in the Soviet Union, but really based more upon the psychology of the mechanistic Russian, Ivan Pavlov.

The failure of the protagonist in *Before Sunrise* to find happiness brought down upon it the anathema of official critics, who found it to be amoral, antisocial, and even pernicious.

The future experiences of Zoshchenko take this chapter beyond its announced limit, but because they are closely linked with what has gone before, they will provide a significant note on which to end. In the postwar tightening of controls, Zoshchenko became the principal victim of attacks by the Party's Central Committee, which under the direction of its powerful whip, Andrei Zhdanov, instructed writers to work under the influence of *partiynost'*, or Party spirit. In 1946 Zhdanov launched a particular onslaught against the magazine *Zvezda* (*Star*), one of the best journals surviving from the Lenin epoch, for providing a platform for such "scum" as Zoshchenko. His offense this time was a story, "Priklyucheniya obezyany" ("The Adventures of a Monkey"), in which the exploits of a little simian, loose in a city, accent the foibles of mankind. To the official critics, this represented a degradation of life in the Soviet state, and the work of a man who, during the Second World War, had engaged in such unhelpful activities as publishing *Before Sunrise*. After "The Adventures of a Monkey," Zoshchenko virtually disappeared from public view, and was apparently still in disgrace when he died in 1958. By an irony which the Chaplinesque figure at the center of so many of his stories would have appreciated, Zoshchenko's collected works were issued in Leningrad in 1960, in an edition whose first printing ran to 150,000 copies.

3

Soviet Theater to the Second World War

1 *Curtain Up on the Old and the New*

The theater, in tsarist times solid and polished but not truly distinguished, brought into the revolutionary era only a few outstanding experiments, among them that of Konstantin Stanislavsky's Moscow Art Theater. But even this group had by 1917 run its course of innovation. Originally rebelling against stage clichés and stilted realism, Stanislavsky led his devoted disciples first through naturalism, then through an infatuation with symbolism, and finally to psychological realism. He made history by introducing the subtler values of Anton Chekhov's plays; in the 1920s the exported "Stanislavsky Method" of inspired realistic direction and action influenced both Broadway and Hollywood. A number of his actors and directors became émigrés, and of these Mikhail Chekhov, Anton's nephew, did some of his most interesting trailblazing in America. But at home, the aging process and the stern Soviet surveillance have for decades frozen the Moscow Art Theater into a pattern of "re-lived experience" that was no longer inspiring.

Before the revolution, the Russian theater was concentrated in Moscow and St. Petersburg, with a few good and well-attended playhouses in such cities as Odessa and Kiev. Elsewhere the equipment was poor, and actors of little skill played to slim audiences. After the revolution, the government realized the propagandistic value of drama and helped to spread theaters across the Soviet Union. Today there are more than three hundred of them (more than thirty in

Moscow alone), with another large number devoted to opera and ballet; and there are several hundred children's theaters.

Soviet drama was at first organized under the People's Commissariat of Education, whose director (1917–29) was Anatoly Lunacharsky. As a playwright himself, he had an intimate understanding of theatrical problems. While vainly waiting for great Marxist plays to appear, the standard companies and the newly organized groups drew upon the old repertory. In Petrograd in 1919, for example, one of the first seriously professional theaters to be established by the Soviets began its career with Schiller's *Don Carlos*, a play about victims of the monarchical system.

Bold experimentation was represented by Vsevolod Meyerhold who, already in his forties and with a background and prestige in the prerevolutionary theater, joined the Communist Party and tried out various avant-garde ideas in his directing. He was not by conviction a Communist (far from it), but he was a revolutionary in theater. His enrollment in the Party was frankly an opportunistic step: he would use his Party privileges and connections to further his sharp innovations on the stage. Even before the revolution he had staged classics with his own changes and additions in their texts; he had sought the satirical and the grotesque; he had brought in masques. Now under the new Red régime his ingenuity would indeed be unbridled.

In 1918 he took over the Petrograd conservatory to stage the first ambitious attempt at original drama since the revolution, the poet Mayakovsky's *Misteriya-buf* (*Mystery-Bouffe*) which, despite praise by Lunacharsky, was a failure. But Mayakovsky rewrote the play, and when Meyerhold produced it again, in Moscow in 1921, it became the first resounding success of the Soviet theater.

Using satire, allegory, and some of the elements of the medieval mystery play, Mayakovsky's *Mystery-Bouffe* projects the terror of the bourgeois at the threat of another world flood: the revolution. But in spite of its initial success, the play never became a permanent part of the repertory of the new state, partly because of the difficulties of staging it and partly because the officials who at first hailed *Mystery-Bouffe* began to notice ideological defects in it; and today the whole thing seems too elementary, as well as bound too topically to its own moment, to capture the interest of audiences. Later, after the theater of the new state was well established, Meyerhold staged Mayakovsky's two other plays, *Klop* (1929; *The Bedbug*) and *Banya* (1930; *The Bathhouse*), both of which violently satirized Soviet bureaucracy, the latter play containing some projections into the future by means of a Wellsian time-machine. The history of these plays reflects the history of the revolutionary theater itself. *The Bedbug* appeared at the end of a period in which the government had permitted literature to criticize it; now the official critics attacked the play, its author, its producer, and even the writer of its music, Dmitry Shostakovich. *The Bathhouse* was even more severely reprimanded. It was during the uproar over this production that Mayakovsky killed himself. The play was withdrawn, and neither it nor *The Bedbug* appeared again in the Russian theater for another quarter-century, until after the death of Stalin.

Meanwhile, as the theater continued to operate, several important producers dominated it. Meyerhold, already mentioned as the producer of Mayakovsky's plays, was an extreme modernist, technically a Constructivist and neo-mechanist: his jungle-gym settings, with their open cubes and encircling ramps, turned most of the plays he staged into spectacles. The actors, and sometimes the playwright, were dwarfed in Meyerhold's productions. On the other hand, Stanislavsky, the one-time associate of Chekhov, insisted on developing, at the Moscow Art Theater, that famous method by which actors could project realistic effects and repeat these in performance after performance. Stanislavsky, while continuing to offer traditional plays, was also a pioneer in staging new dramas of the revolution.

Alexander Tairov, who believed neither in Stanislavsky's systematization of acting nor in Meyerhold's diminishing of it, began in 1914 his long reign at the Kamernyi [Chamber] Theater. Tairov strove to re-create life's exquisite beauty. His productions were punctuated with elegant chants and music and graceful gestures. But in the mid-thirties he made the mistake of satirizing ancient folklore—this at the time when Stalin was harnessing Russian nationalism to Communism. From then on Tairov was mercilessly attacked by the Party, and in 1949 his theater was ordered closed on charges of "alien ideology." He died the next year.

Immediately after the revolution, several dedicated Communist producers had appeared, including Nikolai Okhlopkov (who eventually became director of a playhouse named for the workers' quarter in Moscow, the State Realistic Theater of Red Presnya), Alexander Popov (of the Theater of the Revolution), and Yevgeny Vakhtangov (whose Third Workshop was renamed in his honor after his premature death in 1922).

The growth of Soviet literature into a phase of somewhat free political criticism toward the end of the 1920s has already been referred to. Not that official critics didn't closely follow the Party line and glorify the new state; but from 1925 to 1929, the Central Committee of the Communist Party exercised some tolerance in permitting the kind of self-criticism it felt was necessary for improvement of the country. It was at this time that Formalism developed as a literary philosophy, stressing the techniques and devices of literature and emphasizing symbols and isolating linguistic elements. Party-line doctrinists regarded all this as dangerous art-for-art's-sake esthetics which allowed writers to forget or skip past their Communist obligations. The reaction came in 1929, with Leopold Averbakh heading the Russian Association of Proletarian Writers (RAPP), mentioned in an earlier chapter. Under him the principle of *sotsial'nyi zakaz*, or social command, made literature a part of the Five-Year Plan and shut out fellow travelers and various other individuals or groups which hadn't stringently followed the Party line in their writings; but, as also noted earlier, RAPP's control over authors ended in 1932, when the Union of Soviet Writers, with Gorky as first president, was formed. At this time, *sotsialisticheskiy realizm*, or Socialist realism, became the official doctrine, as it still is. This demands an employment of realism which shows the difficulties of the struggle to establish and maintain the new type of state; the Socialist aspects of the writing must demonstrate the ultimate triumph of the principles of that new state. Seen against the background of these developments, the story of the Soviet drama in the 1920s and '30s is easier to understand.

For decades, propagandistic and patriotic plays, written on the Party's instructions, were in the repertory of all the Soviet theaters. Early in the revolutionary period and again during the Second World War, some of these plays attracted interested and even enthusiastic audiences, particularly when free tickets were issued wholesale to trade unions and schools. But in time, as the revolutionary fevers ebbed in the 1920s and the war ended in 1945, and after the theater administrations were told to show profit, the commercially minded managers preferred Russian and Western classics to Soviet panegyrics. This policy indeed filled the theaters, sometimes to overflowing. More often than not, especially after Stalin's death, the Party could not do much about stopping this trend of profit before propaganda.

2   Some New Kinds of Comedy

Before comedies about the new order began appearing on Russian stages, the informal and amateurish *agitki*, the so-called self-entertainment propagandistic plays, became popular at factories and workers' clubs or in village squares. These *agitki*, informal scenarios generally acted out on an impromptu basis, were ephemeral, but they helped arouse interest in the theater. (And indeed, they were forerunners of the many "improvisational groups" of the Western theaters in the 1960s and '70s.) Gradually, professional Soviet comedy grew behind the *agitki*: comedy showing the villainy of country landlords or the uselessness of the *obyvaleti*, those self-centered misfits from the bourgeois past who hadn't become an integral part of the collective system. One of the most successful of these plays in their early phases was Nikolai Erdman's *Mandat* (1925; *Credentials*), a broad farce poking fun at a rich man who attempts to obtain Party connections through a relation-by-marriage. *Credentials*, vigorously staged by Meyerhold, had plenty of slapstick among all its happy confusions, and it exactly fitted the mood at the time. Its author, Erdman (1902–70), who wrote unpublished but widely circulated epigrams on Stalin and his entourage, was arrested in 1937, but miraculously survived the dictator. Erdman was released in 1954, when he was allowed by Nikita Khrushchev to write again, mostly for the films.

Another comic spectacle of the time was Vladimir Bill-Belotserkovsky's *Burya* (1925; *The Storm*), produced at Moscow's Trade Union Theater. An episodic pageant filled with stock types, it dealt with the struggle of a town to find its Soviet identity at the time of the civil war. A considerably more subtle play dealing with the civil-war period, Konstantin Trenyov's *Lyubov' Yarovaya* (1926) was moved from one of the smaller playhouses to be a thumping success at the Moscow Art Theater. Its name character, a small-town schoolteacher, takes up arms against the husband she loves, who is a White officer. A number of colorful characters appear in this play, including the sailor Shvandaya, who like the heroine is a loyal Bolshevik; but Shvandaya is also a gay rogue and an attractive cheat.

In a quite different kind of comedy, the satirist Boris Romashov ridiculed the Nepmen, the men of the New Economic Policy, who were often racketeers like Rak in this play, *Vozdushnyi pirog* (1925; *The Sweet Soufflé*). The comic novel by Valentin Katayev, *Rastratchiki* (1926; *The Embezzlers*), was mentioned in an earlier chapter; this story of two clerks absconding with some money from a Moscow trust and going on a spree, was also a success when dramatized, but Katayev's greatest fame in the theater came from his comedy, *Kvadvaruta kruga* (1928; *Squaring the Circle*). One of the few Soviet plays to be exported, it was produced in New York in the early 1930s (with the late Glenn Hunter) and in Paris some twenty years later. *Squaring the Circle*, which shows many amusing angles of collectivized living, concerns two young men sharing a one-room apartment who bring home wives and then discover incompatibilities in that the bourgeois-type Ludmila is not happy with the ardent young Communist Vasya, and seeks consolation from Abram; he in turn is not altogether at ease with his bride Tonya, a disciplined and fervent Party member. But the Soviet divorce-and-marriage system makes it possible for the young men to exchange wives easily, thereby squaring the circle. Party ideologues sharply criticized such levity, but the play, which came toward the end of the age of relaxation, had an uproarious popularity.

3   Bulgakov: Triumph and Trouble

One of the more generally serious dramatists of the time, Mikhail Bulgakov (1891–1940), drew sharp censure, even in the time of relaxed criticism, for his *Dni Turbinykh* (1926; *The Days of the Turbins*). This had previously appeared as a two-volume novel, *Belaya gvardiya* (*The White Guard*), based on the experiences of the author in Kiev during that confusing time in 1918 when German troops, Ukrainian nationalists, and Bolsheviks in turn fought for and occupied the city. Bulgakov, who had studied medicine at Kiev but decided to practice literature instead, had drawn criticism in 1923 for his first collection of stories, *Dyaboliada* (*Deviltry*), because it satirized contemporary Russian life. In 1926, the same year as his play *The Days of the Turbins*, Bulgakov's comedy *Zoykina kvartira* (1920; *Zoyka's Apartment*) was banned from the stage, and so was Bulgakov's later satire, *Bagrovyi ostrov* (1927; *The Crimson Island*), which foretold the failure of world revolution. This play also contained some indirect criticism of Soviet censorship, with which Bulgakov was well acquainted.

Despite the heavy criticism of *The Days of the Turbins* on the ground that it showed members of the White army as human beings, and despite a temporary suppression, the play was permitted to continue at the Moscow Art Theater because Stalin himself took up the dramatist's cause. Stalin continued to protect Bulgakov who, when his play *Molière* was banned in 1936, asked permission to leave the country. Stalin refused to let him go and bestowed upon him the Red Banner medal for his services to the Soviet theater. Bulgakov spent his last years as a translator and adapter of plays for the Moscow Art Theater.

It is one of the odd aspects of Soviet literature that writers who have offended official doctrine during their lifetimes, and have been suppressed or imprisoned or executed, are often "rehabilitated" after they have been for some years dead—this has happened even in the case of Ivan Bunin, the voluntary émigré who heaped scorn on Soviet Russia from his vantage point in Paris. In 1956, the Soviets revived Bulgakov, and Moscow's Vakhtangov Theater staged *The Days of the Turbins*.

4 Fighting Plays

Another theatrical triumph of the 1920s, Vsevolod Ivanov's *Bronepoyezd 14–69* (1922–27; *Armored Train No. 14–69*), ran into considerably less opposition. Like Bulgakov's *Turbins*, Ivanov's *Armored Train* had been first a novel. Its author was a member of the Serapion Brothers, that group of individualists which included such noted writers as Mikhail Zoshchenko and Konstantin Fedin. The Brotherhood received encouragement from Gorky, who from the first had sponsored Ivanov, virtually bringing him from vagabondage into literature. In his magazine *Letopis'* (*Annals*), Gorky in 1916 published the young Ivanov's first story, "Po Irtyshu" ("Along the Irtysh River"), but rejected others with the advice that the author needed more experience at living. Ivanov obtained some of this in the Red Army, and after being wounded went to Petrograd in 1920, at the age of twenty-five, to resume his writing career. When he brought out *Armored Train* as a novel in 1922, its success was immediate, for it was a realistic and energetic story of men in battle. Ivanov's next novels, *Tsvetnyie vetry* (1922; *Colored Winds*) and *Golubyie peski* (1923; *Blue Sands*), were formless, exotic books, full of impressionistic portraits of nature: "Outside, the yellow aspen grove mutters; the road is like a golden rag in the wind."

Later in his career, Ivanov repudiated his Serapion background, which had resulted in his frequently being accused of deviation from Party policies; in 1934, he told an all-Soviet literary congress of the need for Communist "tendentiousness." His *Pokhozhdeniya fakira* (1934-35; *The Adventures of a Fakir*) was a novel which reflected his youthful wanderings as a carnival wrestler and sword swallower. In 1936 he attempted a historical play, *Dvenadtsat' molodtsov iz tabakerki* (*Twelve Sturdy Men from a Snuffbox*), dealing with the assassination of Tsar Paul I, but none of Ivanov's later work has the force of his earlier writings. *Armored Train*, which captured and retained the public fancy, is the story of a group of Red guerrillas in the Russian Far East who seize a train loaded with weapons and ammunition belonging to the Whites. Four years after its production at the Moscow Art Theater, *Armored Train* was staged in New York (in 1931). Its most famous line is the ringing cry, "It is for the sake of the truth that our Russia is burning!"

Ivanov's *Armored Train* had elements in common with another famous play of the time, Sergei Tretyakov's *Rychi, Kitai!* (1926; *Roar, China!*), which took a battleship for its setting, and even if this was only scaffolding and lathe, it was effective, and the pivoting of the big guns out over the audience was a bit of stage trickery that spectators thrilled to. Directed with skill by Meyerhold (and also produced in the United States), *Roar, China!* was essentially a kind of sensational parody of some of Mayakovsky's futuristic efforts. *Roar, China!* was written while its author was professor of Russian literature at the National University, Peking, and the play is an attack upon foreign imperialism in that country. Tretyakov, who said that the new state needed "biographies of *things*" and who scolded the fellow-traveler writers for not being more concerned with the future, had a bad future himself: he was later denounced as a Trotskyite and British spy, and during the purges of 1938 he perished, one subsequent explanation being that he had "often met foreign authors," and this had made him suspect in Stalin's eyes.

5   Five-Year-Plan Plays

Most of the plays of the time of the First Five-Year Plan were, like other art forms of the period, concerned with idealizing the industrial and agricultural workers who were successfully overcoming the difficulties confronting them. A few of the dramas of the time rose above the dead level of mere propaganda, among them Vladimir Kirshon's *Khleb* (1930; *Bread*), Alexander Afinogenov's *Strakh* (1931; *Fear*), and Yuri Olesha's *Spisok blagodeyaniy* (1931; *A List of Good Deeds*).

Kirshon, whose first play, *Rzhavchina* (1927; *Rust*), was acted in New York as well as in Moscow, dealt in his later drama, *Bread*, with the problems of the *kolkhoz*, or collective farm, whose deprived peasants have to struggle against the *kulaks*. Kirshon's play, besides dramatizing the efforts of the government to prevent the *kulaks* from taking all the grain for themselves, also projects the antagonism between an icy and correctly oriented Party leader and hysterical colleague who takes "the wrong line." That is what Kirshon himself was eventually accused of doing, for he was arrested in 1937, and was shot in late July 1938, at the age of thirty-six.

Afinogenov, who in 1941 was to be killed at the age of thirty-seven by a German bomb dropped on Moscow, had in the 1920s written some conventional Soviet melodramas, but in *Fear* he struck a deeper note. Originally produced at the Moscow Art Theater, this play had as its central figure old Professor Borodin, possibly modeled on Pavlov, who believed that fear was the dominating motive of citizens in the Communist state. Before the final curtain, however, Borodin discovered that the men of the new order were brave and that it was the tsarists who were afraid; during the play, Borodin had been hoodwinked by spies and saboteurs, against whom he turned at the end, revealing his new loyalty to the new state. This was neat, if not always convincing, drama.

Shortly before he was killed, Afinogenov wrote a play, *Nakanune* (*On the Eve*), first performed in 1942, which concerned the German attack on Russia. (The late Maurice Hindus, in his last book, *A Traveler in Two Worlds* [1971], revealed that Afinogenov once borrowed his King James Bible from him and that later in the 1940s Afinogenov's American-born widow told Hindus "how often her husband had turned to it during the darkest year of his life." For on the eve of his being killed by Hitler's bomb, Stalin's vengeance had threatened him: "*Pravda* had denounced him as an 'enemy of the people,' and he and his family withdrew to the country. He never knew when the night would come that a knock on the door would summon him, perhaps to death from a bullet in the back of his head, the Soviet way of executing political offenders. During those anxious and wakeful nights, one of the books he, a Party member and an atheist, read for forgetfulness and comfort was the Bible he had borrowed from me five years earlier and never returned. I shall always be glad he didn't.")

Olesha in his play *A List of Good Deeds* deals with the problems of the actress Goncharova, who is at first unable to accept the new state without reservations. After playing in *Hamlet*, she carries on intense symbolic discussions about that tragedy and the relationship of the new society to the old. In Paris, in a moment of decision, she takes the side of a Communist in a street brawl and is killed by another émigré who is an agent of the local police. The play, which has moments of great effectiveness, heightened by its recurrent Charles Chaplin theme, is a statement of Olesha's own dilemma. Criticized harshly, he had to "confess his errors" publicly. He wrote little more, and died a deeply unhappy man at sixty-one, in 1960.

Maxim Gorky made two contributions to the Soviet theater in the 1930s, the first two parts of a trilogy he didn't live to complete: *Yegor Bulychev i drugiye* (1932; *Yegor Bulychev and Others*) and *Dostigayev i drugiye* (1933; *Dostigayev and Others*). The first of these was a pronounced success at the Vakhtangov Theater and later at the Moscow Art Theater and throughout Russia. *Bulychev* is the story of a wealthy merchant dying of cancer amid the events of the revolutionary year 1917; he has no illusions about tsarism or the bourgeois class of which he has become a part through his moneymaking, and he virtually welcomes the rise of the Bolsheviks. It is a complicated play, ironic and often comic, and crowded with interesting characters. Its sequel, *Dostigayev,* was far less successful artistically and with the public. The play, whose action takes place after Bulychev's death, shows the shady political maneuverings of his former partner, Dostigayev. As a play, *Dostigayev* lacks the dramatic force of *Bulychev,* with its believable human conflicts and its satiric strength. As noted earlier, Gorky never wrote drama or fiction about life under the Soviet régime, though these two dramas anticipate it.

On the other hand, the novelist Leonid Leonov wrote several important plays about Soviet life after successfully dramatizing his first novel, *Barsuki (The Badgers)* in the 1920s—*The Badgers* dealt only with the beginnings of the new state. But Leonov treated contemporary Soviet existence in such plays of the 1930s as *Polovchanskiye sady* (1936–38; *The Orchards of Polovchansk*), *Volk* (1938; *The Wolf,* also known as *Begstvo Sandukova, The Flight of Sandukov*), and *Obyknovennyi chelovek* (1940–41; *An Ordinary Man*). *The Orchards of Polovchansk,* produced at the Moscow Art Theater, is a reunion of the Makkaveyev family, whose head is the director of a state orchard. In its earlier version, the play had a Chekhovian quality, as the title suggests, but as Leonov rewrote it he cheapened it somewhat by making the climax of the drama the exposure (at a family reunion) of a friend who turns out to be an enemy agent. *The Wolf* also deals with the unmasking of secret enemies and similarly has a family background; the element of claptrap is even more intrusive than in the other play. *An Ordinary Man* is a satiric comedy about a braggart who suggests that an old friend he hasn't seen for a long time, who comes for a visit, should pretend to be important in order to impress the host's neighbors. The joke of course is that the visitor has really become an important man, a distinguished scientist and high-ranking Party member.

6   Other Comedies of the Thirties

Leonov's wartime dramas will be considered later; here, some of the comedies by other playwrights will be discussed. One of these men is Veniamin Kaverin (pen name of Veniamin Zilber), born in 1902 and a member of the Serapion group. He began his career by writing stories that combined the romantic and the grotesque, and in his novel *Khudozhnik neizvesten* (1927–28; *Artist Unknown*) he portrayed a man not adjusted to the new technical society, who, even in defeat, preserves his integrity. Kaverin had a somewhat different outlook in his famous comedy, *Ukroshcheniye mistera Robinsona ili poteryannyi rai* (1933; *The Taming of Mr. Robinson, or Paradise Lost*). Mr. Robinson is an aging English chemist who has his family with him in the Soviet Union; he leaves them to find happiness in working for the new state. One of the high points of the comedy is Robinson's dialogue, conducted as he drinks rum and cognac, with a Humpty-Dumpty figure that seems to stand for the comically divergent Robinson family. Another comedy about a foreigner, this time a Frenchman, is an operetta by Nikolai Aduyev, *Kak yeyo zovut?* (1935; *What Is Her Name?*), the story of an imported young architect who, after several love affairs, marries a Russian girl and settles in to become a constructive member of the new society.

Some of these later comedies, like those of the twenties, have *kolkhoz*, or collective-farm, backgrounds. In Aleksei Simukov's *Svad'ba* (1935; *The Wedding*), two lovers find that belonging to different collective farms is an obstacle to their marriage—for a while. *Bogataya nevesta* (1936; *The Rich Bride*), by Ilya Ilf and Yevgeny Petrov in collaboration with Petrov's brother, Valentin Katayev, deals with the love affair between a *kolkhoz* girl and a sailor in the Red Navy. All these plays are light and hardly of permanent importance; they are entertaining views of Soviet life which don't offend the Party critics.

Some other comedies of the 1930s which might be mentioned are those by Viktor Gusev, Vasily Shkvarkin, and Konstantin Finn. The first of these men was noted for his folk-type songs which, along with those of the poet Mikhail Isakovsky, were extremely popular with peasant choirs and army choruses. Gusev's *Slava* (1934–35; *Glory*) shows a girl deciding that her true love is not the man who hoped to perform a heroic deed for the sake of glory, but rather a man who did perform a heroic deed for the sake of the people and in spite of his own terror. Shkvarkin's *Nochnoi smotr* (1937; *Night Review*), like Gusev's *Glory*, mingles the serious with the comic; in *Night Review*, a schoolmaster who saves a girl from drowning must decide whether he loves her or his wife, a dilemma the play doesn't resolve. Similarly, in Finn's *Svidaniye* (1935; *Rendezvous*), an engineer is in love with two women and, after the one of them who is married leaves him, he takes up with the other, a pretty telegraph operator; these and several additional characters finally work together in a *kolkhoz* for the glory of the new state.

7 The Successes of Pogodin

A consistently successful playwright from the 1920s on, Nikolai Pogodin (1900–1962), was a Don River peasant's son, born Nikolai Stukalov. He worked as farmhand and blacksmith's assistant before going into journalism and, eventually, into imaginative writing. His plays, which deal with the common man rather than the inward-looking, questing type of hero, never involved him in trouble with the custodians of thought. *Temp* (1929; *Tempo*), staged by Nikolai Okhlopokov at the Realistic Theater, shows how the Stalingrad tractor plant was constructed in spite of laggards and saboteurs. In the course of the play, which was written before the plant was actually finished, an American engineer learns to admire Soviet methods. *Poema o topore*

(1930; *Poem of the Ax*), similar to the earlier play in character and situation, was produced at the Theater of the
Revolution by Aleksei Popov; it concerns the fabrication of
nonrusting steel. *Sneg* (1932; *Snow*) is the dramatization of
the problems of an exploring party in the Caucasus where,
as they battle against the forces of nature, several of the
characters come to see the virtues of Communism. *Moy
drug* (1932; *My Friend*), Pogodin's first play after the
Writers' Union decreed the necessity for Socialist realism,
fitted neatly into the approved pattern, as his earlier dramas
had. This one, also staged by Popov, featured a factory director who was perhaps an even more positive type than
Pogodin's former heroes.

His *Posle bala* (1933; *After the Ball*), which begins and
ends with a Strauss waltz, has lighter elements in it but
also a far more tragic aspect in the suicide of a girl who
kills herself because of circumstances arising partly out of
the fact that the *kolkhoz* she directs is being betrayed by
her father. In Pogodin's greatest success, *Aristokraty* (1934-
35; *Aristocrats*), he makes comedy out of a basically serious
situation, the use of prisoners to help construct the canal
from the White Sea to the Baltic. Pogodin, in a cinematic
flashing of episodes, deals with some of the harsher concentration-camp realities, but avoids showing most of the evils
connected with the building of that canal. These evils were
well known in Russia at the time: the floggings, the in-
adequate hospitalization, the wretched clothing of the laborers, the high death rate, and the lack of communication with
the world outside. Pogodin in *Aristocrats* concerned himself
mostly with the rehabilitation of his characters, particularly
with that of a thief with possibilities of constructive leadership. Nikolai Okhlopokov's Realistic Theater effectively
staged the play which, if it didn't tell the whole truth about
its situation, at least presented a lively gallery of characters,
chiefly from the underworld, who became transformed into
aristocrats of labor.

Pogodin followed with two resoundingly popular plays
about Lenin: *Chelovek s ruzhyom* (1937; *The Man with
the Gun*) and *Kremlyovskiye kuranty* (1940, rewritten in

1955; *The Kremlin Chimes*). The first of these is about a peasant soldier who meets Lenin. The second, *The Kremlin Chimes*, is partly about an old Jewish watchmaker whose ambition is to make the Kremlin bells play the "Internationale." This play came out in the year Hitler attacked Russia; the wartime and postwar career of Pogodin, which continued his earlier successes, will be taken up later.

8   The End of a Phase

As the 1930s drew to a close, the techniques of production were changing in the Soviet theaters. The great creative epoch of production had passed. Classic repertory continued to hold the stage; indeed, directors often preferred its comparative safety to risking new plays which might prove to be controversial. Managers had to be particularly careful of their ideology after Hitler's attack, which brought on what in Russia was known as the Great Patriotic War. And even after peace came, restrictions were still severe during the last years of Stalin's régime.

In 1938 Stanislavsky died at seventy-five; Stanislavsky, who had invented one age of the theater and had adapted himself to another. Some other producers, like some other writers, didn't have his ability to survive—Meyerhold, for example. In 1938, after arguments and scandals, the state closed the theater which was named for Meyerhold; once a Party functionary, he apparently hadn't kept abreast of shifts in Party ideology—he was indeed too revolutionary for Stalin. His old rival, Stanislavsky, to his eternal credit, just before his death offered Meyerhold a job which he didn't take. But Meyerhold appeared at the first all-Soviet congress of theater producers on June 15, 1939 and gave a speech. On the night of the 17th he was arrested; then, like so many others, he disappeared. Shortly afterward, his actress wife, Zinaida Raikh (formerly married to Sergei Yesenin), was murdered in her apartment, stabbed from head to foot with seventeen knife wounds, her eyes cut out, her throat slashed open. Police said this must have been the

work of an unknown tramp. The outside world didn't hear
of Meyerhold again until 1958, when the *Great Soviet Encyclopedia* reported that he had died in 1942, though precisely how was not explained. A yet later report has it that
he was executed in Moscow on February 2, 1940, after a
prolonged and hideous torture.

What had he said at the convention of theater producers
in June 1939? He had bluntly declared that recent Soviet
productions were colorless and tedious, with little true
theater art in them. This was, he told his audience, the
fault of Socialist realism, which was pitiful and sterile. He
hit out fearlessly:

> Where only a short time ago the creative thought pulsed
> like a lively spring, where men of art in their search, in
> their errors, often stumbling and turning off the path,
> nevertheless did create and did build things that were
> sometimes bad but sometimes splendid; where the world's
> best theaters existed—now there reigns because of you
> something depressing, something "decent" yet so average,
> something that shocks and kills by its very talentless
> essence. Is that what you were striving for? If so, what a
> frightful result did you achieve! Wishing to throw the
> dirty water out, you also threw out the child along with
> it. Gunning after formalism you have destroyed art!

By one of those ironies of Soviet Russian history, Meyerhold was in 1956 posthumously rehabilitated, and his notes
and sketches were collected.

9 Soviet Films: Eisenstein

The wide recognition gained in the West by "the
Method" of Konstantin Stanislavsky's theater was matched
by the innovations of Sergei Eisenstein's cinema. His films
were hailed in Europe and America as a high triumph
achieved despite the Party's control and terror, and notwithstanding the ever present command to propagandize.

In the early days of Eisenstein (who was toward the end

of his career in official disfavor), Western liberals were indeed willing to lend a sympathetic eye to his films, which used new techniques to produce what amounted to a new kind of folk art that expressed the needs and aspirations of a people. His evocation of the great naval revolt of 1905 on the Black Sea was notable in this respect. Known in Russia as *Bronenosets Potyomkin* [Battleship Potyomkin], the film is famous in the West as *Potemkin.*

If there was propaganda in Eisenstein's pictures of the 1920s, it often seemed a justifiable and organic part of the stories being presented: the sailors aboard the *Potemkin* had actually been given maggoty meat, and tsarst troops had really cut down the people on the Odessa waterfront steps. Esenstein made of the latter episode one of the greatest film scenes, while in *Oktyabr'* (1927; *Ten Days That Shook the World*), his employment of montage was particularly effective.

In that picture Eisenstein showed that, in true Soviet fashion, he had little use for the man who had been head of the state after the tsar's abdication—Alexander Kerensky —and little for the right-wing general—Lavr Kornilov—who led an abortive mutiny in August 1917. But whatever the ideological bias, the film was masterly in its use of cinematic imagery, particularly in the scene which showed the statuette of Napoleon in Kerensky's room; then, as Kerensky and Kornilov were projected in an imaginary confrontation, the statuette was in its turn confronted by its double, so that the two men and the two figures of Napoleon moved toward one another in opposition. Many Western liberals, accepting the art of this and of other Soviet films, believed they were holding the propaganda at arm's length, but in many cases it was sliding into their consciousness.

Soviet films indeed, in the 1920s and '30s, won worldwide renown thanks to bold directors such as Sergei Eisenstein and Vsevolod Pudovkin. Both are said to have considerably influenced the Hollywood of that time, mostly in the areas of montage, stereoscopy, and color photography. Yet the deeper worth of their films may now be seriously questioned. The verdict of history may well be that the Soviet moviemaking of that period was vastly—propagandistically—over-rated. Even Eisenstein's epochal *Potemkin* made in 1925 can now, in a more sober light, be seen as excessively dramatic. His *Alexander Nevsky* of 1938 owed more to Sergei Prokofyev's score than to any artistic veracity of Eisenstein's direction, although the battle scenes showed the historic enough defeat of the Teutonic knights, by thirteenth-century Russians, at Lake Peipus. When Eisenstein tried for a truer expression, his 1935–37 film *Bezhin lug* (*The Bezhin Meadow*), based on Turgenev's story, was banned by Stalin. Because Eisenstein died in 1948, five years before Stalin, we can never know the real heights of his talent.

4

Soviet Poetry Between the Civil War and the Second World War

1   Tikhonov, Bedny, and Bezymensky

Several of the poets who were writing at the time of the revolution and just after it have been discussed earlier; now some of those who wrote between that period and the Second World War will be considered. The outstanding figure of this group is Boris Pasternak who, although he began publishing before the First World War and continued after the Second, did much of his important work in the interim; he will be discussed in a later section.

After Pasternak, one of the most important poets of Soviet Russia is Nikolai Tikhonov (1896–). He has certain background elements in common with Zoshchenko; like him, Tikhonov served in the tsar's army in the First World War, later fighting for the Reds in the civil war and subsequently becoming one of the Serapion Brothers. Unlike Zoshchenko, however, Tikhonov avoided trouble with the authorities. A man who believes that a writer's work should be politically oriented, he has invariably won official approval for it. This doesn't mean that he is a Party-line hack, for he has written some fine poetry and fiction, even if it is not of the first rank.

In his postrevolutionary verse, Tikhonov was greatly influenced by the prewar credo of the group which had established the doctrine of Acmeism, whose ideal—as already pointed out—was not the suggestiveness of the Symbolists but concreteness. Their leader had been Nikolai Gumilyov (1886–1921), who had originally felt the attraction of the Symbolist method; after being decorated for bravery fighting against the Germans in the First World War, he lectured and conducted writing workshops for the new Soviet régime, which executed him after finding him guilty of taking part in a conspiracy.

This was in 1921, the year Tikhonov joined the Serapion Brothers and the year before he brought out his first book of verse, *Orda* (1922; *The Horde*). This collection of war poems revealed the Acmeist influence of Gumilyov in its preference for nouns, in its precision and tangibility. Consider this stanza from Tikhonov's *Horde* poem, "Koni" ("The Horses"):

> *Life instructed me with rifle and with oar,*
> *While the knotted cords of a strong wind*
> *Lashed hard on my shoulders,*
> *To make me at once more skillful and more calm,*
> *And plain as nails of iron.*

As in *The Horde*, civil-war themes predominate in Tikhonov's next book of poetry, *Braga* (1923; *Brew*), whose narrative verse often resembles the ballad style of Kipling. Tikhonov turned to fiction in the late 1920s and wrote several remarkable stories, including "Riskovannyi chelovek" (1927; "The Reckless Man"). His novel *Voina* (1931; *War*) is concerned with the origin of the use of poison gas; and the gas mask is one of the most striking images of Tikhonov's long poem of Europe on the edge of war, *Ten' druga* (1935; *The Shade of a Friend*), which also deals with the Italians in Abyssinia, the miners of Spain, the victims of Nazi atrocities, and various other eve-of-war manifestations in the countries of Western Europe. Tikhonov's later career is deeply bound up with the Second World War which he envisioned, and with its aftermath.

An older poet than Tikhonov, Yefim Pridvorov (1883–1945), wrote under the name of Demyan Bedny (Damian the Poor). Bedny, who became a kind of poet laureate of the Soviet state, was an ardent Bolshevik even in tsarist times, when he wrote not only advertising ditties about tobacco for a living, but also subtle revolutionary propaganda in the guise of Aesop-like fables. After the revolution he liked to stress his peasant origins and wrote plain, coarse-humored verses which had a wide popularity and helped spread pro-Soviet sentiments throughout the land. But although Bedny was a favorite of Stalin's, he got into trouble in 1936 with his comic opera, *Bogatyri* (*Ancient Heroes*), which made fun of the Christianizing of Russia in the tenth century; Bedny's intended-to-be-hilarious version of this was that everyone was drunk at the time. An official frown came from the Kremlin: with a pan-European war expected, the Party was reviewing its relations with the Church and deciding that the latter's influence had been a good one in earlier Russia; Karl Marx had said as much. Besides, Bedny in his libretto seemed to be mocking the venerated heroes of old. So the play was removed, and little more was heard of Bedny from that time until the news of his death in 1945. (It is interesting to note that in the early 1920s Carl Sandburg was sufficiently captivated by Bedny's verses to have them translated into English for him. He meant to put them into his own words and rhythms, but fortunately never did. For surely Bedny's limited effusions were not worth Sandburg's gifts.)

Of but a slightly higher caliber was Alexander Bezymensky (1898–1973). He came from a middle-class family and joined the Bolsheviks in 1917. His ardent Communist poetry in the early 1920s was published with prefaces by Trotsky. The poet tried to live this down after Stalin's ascendance by zealously putting the Party line into practically every poem he wrote. He borrowed from Mayakovsky's style but denounced the master's suicide in his rather uninspired verses. During the purges of the 1930s he castigated the victims as he eulogized Stalin. One of his most shocking performances was his poem in June 1937 in praise of the execution of Marshal Mikhail Tukhachevsky and his associates. But in this bloodthirsty verse-making he was not so ingenuous as Bedny who at the time, in his fifty-four-line poem on the same subject, managed to include all the victims' names in his rhymes.

2   Aseyev: Bemedaled Bohemian

Nikolai Aseyev (1889–1963), a disciple of Mayakovsky, was a city bohemian in, of all places, Vladivostok. His first volume of verse, *Nochnaya fleita* (1914; *Nocturnal Flute*), was written there four years before he went to Moscow. His *Oksana* (1916; Oksana is a female Ukrainian name) was full of extravagant poetic images, such as the one envisioning a cabaret in the sky, where "the moon rested half-naked on a dark-blue chaise lounge," waited on by stars that served oysters. Aseyev, doing his best to be a joiner, celebrated, in *Poema o Budyonnom* (1922; *The Poem about Budyonny*) and similar works, the sucesses of the new state. Because Aseyev had a hatred of the bourgeois that was a holdover from his youthful days as a dedicated bohemian, he disliked the partial return to capitalism represented by the New Economic Policy of 1921; the poem he wrote about his disillusionment he called "Liricheskoye otstupleniye" (1924; "Lyrical Digression"), which included the lines:

> How can I sing for
> This new Communist clan
> When our time is merely carroty,
> Though you call it red?

Aseyev, however, adjusted himself to the new life and turned out a great deal of hackwork, even attempting an epic of the revolution and civil war, *Semyon Proskakov* (1928). In 1939, the Soviet government celebrated the twenty-fifth anniversary of the publication of *Nocturnal Flute* and awarded its author the Order of Lenin. In 1936–39, Aseyev recalled the past in his long portrait-poem, *Mayakovsky nachinayetsya* (*Mayakovsky Begins*), which contains these stanzas:

> In those early times
> There were pride and wonder,

> And horse-drawn streetcars
> Ran along the avenues.
> My friends gathered about me
> On all sides;
> Whichever way I looked,
> I saw a man.
>
> . . . .
>
> He walked along,
> Wide-shouldered, trim,
> Improbable visitor
> From another world,
> Tall as a banner
> Screened against
> The clear sky of June
> Unfurled in splendor.

Despite his Order of Lenin, Aseyev received an official reprimand during the Second World War for having made, in various poems, what the official critics called ideological mistakes.

3 Bryusov and Others

The postrevolutionary career of Valery Bryusov (1873–1924) was unique in the fact that he, a Symbolist, was the only leading member of the prerevolutionary advance-guard groups who joined the Communist Party and received a high government post (in education). Bryusov did his best work early in his career; his last notable book was *Stephanos* (1906). He wrote of the revolution enthusiastically but not well. To show its appreciation, the Moscow government in 1973 ordered the issue of the first full collection of Bryusov's works in six volumes, including not only his poems but also his three novels and many of his literary essays. His Western admirers had anticipated the Soviets in 1971 when in England and Germany some ten books of Bryusov were reprinted in their original Russian, though in limited editions.

In contrast to Bryusov, who tried to accommodate the Soviets, we have the work of two of his more rebellious contemporaries: Nikolai Klyuyev (1887–1937) and the already mentioned (see "Émigré Literature") Vladislav Khodasevich (1886–1939).

Khodasevich, at first attracted by the Russian Symbolists, increasingly inclined to the classical, notably in *Tyazholaya lira* (1922; *The Heavy Lyre*). This was published in the year when he moved to Paris, for in spite of his having been influenced by Bryusov and having been a close friend of Gorky's, Khodasevich disliked the revolution. As an émigré in France, although writing excellent reviews and profound essays as formerly, he changed his style in poetry by producing mainly witty satiric verse.

Klyuyev on the other hand stayed on in Russia. A peasant poet like his friend Yesenin, Klyuyev had links with the Symbolists. He had welcomed the revolution, and in his long poem *Lenin* (1924) he approached the leader of the new state in a religious mood, even comparing him to the Archpriest Avvakum, a heroic martyr of the seventeenth century. But, like Yesenin, Klyuyev never felt completely at home in the postrevolutionary years; the critics denounced him as the poet of the *kulaks*. He was arrested and exiled to Siberia. He died in 1937 of typhus on a train bringing him from the concentration camp after he had served his sentence.

Eduard Bagritsky didn't bring out his first volume of poems until 1928, and since he died in 1934, most of his important work falls in the between-wars period. Bagritsky, whose birth date is sometimes given as 1895 and sometimes as 1897, was actually Eduard Dzyubin, and like the parents of Boris Pasternak he came from the cultivated Jewish colony in Odessa, though from a poorer family. A Red guerrilla in the civil war, Bagritsky in the 1920s became one of the Constructivists who, without sharing the Futurists' contempt for tradition, joined them in admiration of techniques. Further, Constructivists were stylists who believed in making the images and rhythms within a poem conform to a consistent organizational structure, centered in the meaning of the work, as when another poet, Boris Agapov, in a poem whose

setting was a government office, wrote of brows that resembled the signature of the director of the trust.

Bagritsky, who collected all his early verses in *Yugozapad*
(1928; *Southwest*), was not always strictly a Constructivist,
since his temperament was unwaveringly romantic, and although he never seemed to accept the revolution inwardly,
official critics approved of his *Duma pro Opanasa* (1926; *The
Elegy on Opanas*). This is a poetic narrative about the
peasant Opanas, captured by Ukrainian Anarchists and
forced to kill Kogan, a Red leader whom he admires and
tries to induce to escape; later, when Opanas is caught by the
Reds he admits carrying out the execution and stoically con-
fronts his own. The poem draws upon folk songs of the
Ukraine and effectively evokes the landscapes of that
southern region.

The civil war as fought in another area, Eastern Russia, is
narrated in the work of one of the founders of the Constructivist group, Ilya Selvinsky (1899–1968), in *Ulyalayev-
shchina* (1927; *The Ulyalayev Band*). This poem also pits
Communists against Anarchists, with Ulyalayev, the unruly
and banditlike leader of the Anarchists, shown as being no
match for the Communist leader and finally being shot by
his own men, who in a crisis revert to their peasant tendency
to respect property rights. Selvinsky's other notable work is
the verse drama, *Pao-Pao* (1932), whose clowning resembles
that of Zoshchenko's "The Adventures of a Monkey," though
from a somewhat different point of view. Selvinsky's *Pao-Pao*
is an ape who stands for the lower instincts of man as well
as for bourgeois culture itself, but he rises toward the human
plane when introduced into the harmonious atmosphere of a
Soviet factory.

Andrei Platonov (1899–1951), the son of a railroad-shop
worker, himself a worker since the age of fifteen who par-
ticipated in the civil war as a Red Army soldier, wrote poems
and some prose which were at first full of industrial themes
and Communist loyalty. In the mid-1920s a member of the
Pereval (the Divide) group, Platonov subsequently left it
and wrote fiction that Party-line critics rebuked severely.
Platonov's finest work was his historical tale, "Yepifanskiye
shlyuzy" (1927; "The Yepifan Canal Locks"), the story of

an Englishman whom Peter the Great brings to Russia—an engineer who is tricked by native charlatans and who is finally executed by the tsar. Nor did the author escape his own tragedy. Hounded by the Soviet government for his increasingly daring poetry and prose, Platonov was deprived of his right to earn a living as a writer. For many years till his death at the height of Stalinist repression, Platonov was employed as a janitor at the Moscow Literary Institute—the only connection with literature left to him by the almighty Communist Party.

Pavel Vasilyev, a peasant poet like Yesenin and Klyuyev, was among those who tried to join the Soviet stream, and eventually to protest. A writer of vigorous lyrics, he died prematurely in 1937 at the age of twenty-six, when he was shot in prison for his fearless speaking up in defense of the purge victims of the time.

Among the "inner émigrés," that is to say those Russian writers who remained in the country after the revolution but did not welcome it, Maximilian Voloshin (1877–1932) is an outstanding example. A man of great erudition, a mystic, an aesthetic poet of the Symbolist school, he traveled and lived in Western Europe extensively before the First World War, wrote exquisite poems, and translated French poets with consummate skill. In early postrevolution times he tried to seclude himself at Koktebel, on the Crimean shore, but fellow poets and other admirers sought him out, compelling him to hold a kind of cautious and exclusive court. His poems in 1919–25 were of demons and terror; he also tried to evaluate the disturbing present in terms of Russian history. Sadly recognizing the revolution as part of Russia's heavy destiny, he kept apart during the Soviet years until his death.

4 Mandelshtam: The Dilemma of an Intellectual

Disapproval by the caretakers of poetry was the constant lot of Osip Mandelshtam, who in recent years has emerged as one of the great modern Russian writers. He was born in St. Petersburg in 1891; the circumstances of his death, whose date is set by his widow Nadezhda as between December 1938 and April 1939, are not known, but the most probable story about it is that he died of typhus in a transit concentration camp near Vladivostok. His poetry was already widely known among the younger generation of readers.

Mandelshtam, shy and impractical son of a Jewish merchant, brought out in 1913 a volume of twenty quiet and disciplined poems, *Kamen'* (*Stone*). He identified himself with the Acmeist group which lasted from 1912 to the First World War. After the loudness of that event and of the revolution and civil war, Mandelshtam brought out another book of poetry which contrasted with the noise and hysteria of the time: *Tristia* (1922). The opening lines of the title poem convey the quiet melancholy of the book:

> *I have practiced leavetaking in the sorrow of night*
> *Among the loose flowing of a woman's hair.*

Mandelshtam also wrote prose in *Shum vremeni* (1925; *The Sound of Time*), a volume largely reminiscential of his childhood in the stately atmosphere of end-of-the-century St. Petersburg; he subsequently expanded this book somewhat and reissued it as *Yegipetskaya marka* (1928; *The Egyptian Stamp*). His last book of verse, *Stikhotvoreniya* (1928; *Poems*), reprinted his first two and added a score of poems. In one of them, "Vek" ("The Age"), he expressed his despair in his most famous lines:

> *Your spinal cord is broken,*
> *My beautiful, pitiable century.*

A noted saying of Mandelshtam's, "I have never been anyone's contemporary," indicates his dissatisfaction with the revolution; by this he meant that his poems really belong outside this broken-backed century. In the story which gave its name to the volume *The Egyptian Stamp*, Mandelshtam portrayed an intellectual out of key with the new system who outwardly submits to it but secretly maintains contempt for it. This may have been somewhat the plight of Mandel-

shtam, whose opposition took over in his writing. He and
his wife were first arrested and exiled because he had, like
Catullus in the case of Caesar, written an epigram against
Stalin. Caesar was forgiving, but Stalin played his horrible
cat-and-mouse game. On one early occasion he spared Mandelshtam's life after telephoning Boris Pasternak, who as-
sured him that Mandelshtam was a fine poet. Later, however, Stalin changed his mind and doomed Mandelshtam.

His widow survived to write her remarkable reminiscences
and bitter reflections (available in English as *Hope Against
Hope* and *Hope Abandoned*, 1970 and 1974—her name
Nadezhda being the Russian equivalent of Hope). In late
1973 a limited edition of 30,000 copies of Osip Mandelshtam
was printed by the State Literature Publishing House in
Moscow. It had been promised and prepared in the early
1960s but was kept from the presses all this time on the
government's orders. When finally, in December 1973, it
appeared, the entire edition was snapped up by buyers in the
bookstores and at once became a bibliographic rarity.

5   Akhmatova: Tragedy of Great Talent

One of Russia's foremost poets, with a contribution
most refined and a life utterly tragic, was Anna Akhmatova
(1888–1966; real name Anna Gorenko). She was one of the
Acmeist group that flourished between 1912 and 1917, and
for a time she was married to Nikolai Gumilyov, founder of
the movement, whom she divorced in 1918. Anna Akhmatova then married the poet and Assyriologist, Vladimir
Shileyko; as already noted, Gumilyov was shot by a firing
squad in 1921 for taking part in an anti-Soviet plot. Akhmatova was often censured by Party-line critics.

She began writing poetry in childhood. Her first book was
Vecher (1912; *Evening*), a series of delicate lyrics in a language of great musical clarity, with motifs of loneliness and
sorrow. This volume was followed by *Chyotki* (1914; *Prayer
Beads*), *Belaya staya* (1917; *The White Flock*), *Podorozhnik*
(1921; *The Thorn Tree*), *Anno Domini* (1921), and *Stikhi*

(1922; *Verses*). Soviet critics found her personal lyricism not up to what they determined were Marxian standards of literature for the people, and she was often reprimanded in the press. After 1922 she was silent for many years, but at long last—shortly before the Second World War—some of her poems appeared in the Leningrad magazine *Zvezda* (*The Star*), and a book of her earlier verse (written between 1922 and 1938) was published. During the early 1940s some of her war poems came out in print. Later her famous *Requiem*, created between 1935 and 1940, was a literary event of magnitude. In prose she published several studies of Pushkin.

At times her poetry was under official Soviet displeasure and even ban. Her only son was arrested, and she wrote some of her finest lines about her long and soul-wrenching wait with other women in her situation at prison gates to learn of their men's fate. We will return to Akhmatova in speaking of Russian war poems, and again in treating the post-Stalinist "Thaw."

6   Tsvetayeva: End of an Epoch

The death of another poet, Marina Tsvetayeva, distinctly sets the seal on the age of between-wars poetry. Born in Moscow in 1892, daughter of a professor of philology and art at the University, Marina Tsvetayeva went to school in Switzerland and Germany, and in Paris attended lectures at the Sorbonne. In prerevolutionary Russia she became a poet with the volumes *Vecherniy al'bom* (1910; *Evening Album*), *Volshebnyi fonar'* (1912; *The Magic Lantern*), and *Iz dvukh knig* (1913; *From Two Books*). She left Russia after the civil war, in which her husband had been an officer in the White Army. While in Paris she brought out *Versty* (1922; *Milestones*), which greatly impressed Pasternak. He had met her in Russia, through Ilya Ehrenburg, and had not thought highly of her; later he came to see her as a brilliant poet, far more successful at symbolism than most of the other Russian Symbolists. Her work in subsequent books continued to be excellent in its fiery, uneven, short-lined, and highly inventive ways: *Razluka* (1922; *Parting*), *Stikhi k Bloku* (1922; *Poems to Blok*), *Molodets* (1923; *A Fine Fellow*).

Like Pasternak, Marina Tsvetayeva loved the Russian earth and in France and Czechoslovakia felt cut off from her roots; she asked Pasternak's advice about returning in the late 1930s, and he didn't encourage her. Exceedingly bad luck pursued her and her family. Her husband had become a Red secret police agent in Western Europe, returned to the Soviet Union, and disappeared. Their daughter went to their native land to look for him, and was also lost. The poetess with the rest of the family left France for the homeland in 1939. Later it became known that her husband had been executed by Stalin's secret police, and the girl sent to a concentration camp (where she was to spend sixteen years). Marina Tsvetayeva was banished to the provinces, where poor, unpublished, and unable to obtain even menial employment, she hanged herself (August 31, 1941). Her son was killed in battle. Pasternak later wrote, "The tragedy of this family infinitely exceeded all my fears."

5

Russia at War

1 The Soviet Wartime Novel

On June 22, 1941 — just after the summer solstice —
Germany, whose Nazi rulers said they wanted a place in the
sun, attacked Russia, the country with whom they had signed
a nonaggression pact less than two years before, at that time
making possible Germany's movement into Poland which
started the Second World War.

The nation's ferments and torments during the Second
World War provided some of the surviving Soviet writers
with themes and material of patriotic pathos and humane
commiseration. The spirit that inspired Russia's armed
forces in their resistance and in their counterthrusts also inspired the makers of literature, within of course the rigidly
defined limits of censorship. For this heroic time failed to
give these novelists and poets any true surcease from the
Party's harsh edict of what and how to write. Nevertheless,
even while obeying those decrees, the writers of Soviet Russia poured out more spontaneously patriotic literature than
any other nation: only France, with an Aragon and an
Eluard, writing from the underground, was close to Russia in
this matter.

Novels abounded. Even before Russia was attacked it had
its story of involvement, Nikolai Shpanov's short novel,
Pervyi udar (1939; *The First Blow*). This fanciful little book
described the first day of the new war, in which the German
forces would be joined by the Polish to attack the Soviet
Union while England stood by in neutrality. The plot concerns a Soviet bomb attack on Nuremberg. It is highly suc-

cessful and, as the story ends, the planes are ready to go out on another raid. The novel was withdrawn, several months after its appearance, presumably because of the Soviet-Nazi pact. Shpanov later published the novel *Podzhigateli* (1950; *The Incendiaries*), which blames the Western democracies for having brought on the Second World War.

Historical novels emphasizing the greatness of the Russian past became extremely popular during that war. Valentin Kostylyov's *Ivan Groznyi* (1941–45; *Ivan the Terrible*) kept place alongside plays of the period by Aleksei Tolstoy and Vladimir Solovyov attempting to improve the reputation of an early Russian ruler. Tolstoy's own *Pyotr Pervyi* (1931–45; *Peter the Great*) is an important trilogy whose third volume appeared just after the author's death. In part of Sergei Sergeyev-Tsensky's cycle, *Preobrazheniye* (*Transfiguration*), the setting is the First World War: *Brusilovsky proryv* (1943; *Brusilov's Breakthrough*), *Pushki vyduigayut* (1944; *The Guns Are Rolled Out*), and *Pushki zagovorili* (1945; *The Guns Have Spoken*). For supposedly dealing softly with "imperialists," Sergeyev-Tsensky met with official criticism.

The Russian war with Japan was the subject of Alexander Stepanov's prosaic *Port-Arthur* (1944), while Vyacheslav Shishkov's *Pugachov* (1943–44) presented a vigorous portrait of the famous eighteenth-century rebel. But the interest of Russian readers was certainly not focused exclusively on the past.

An extremely interesting novel written directly out of the events it portrays, Ilya Ehrenburg's *Padeniye Parizha* (1941; *The Fall of Paris*) has a curious history. Because Ehrenburg began it before the German attack upon Russia, the book is in two phases. The first section had been printed in the magazine *Znamya* (*Banner*) before the Germans turned eastward. Ehrenburg had been in Paris and had witnessed the French collapse. His Communists in the first part of the story had, under the spell of the Nazi-Soviet pact, been saying it wasn't their war; after Ehrenburg returned to Russia, however, and his country was at war with Germany, he began to portray his French Communists as the true French patriots. The book, despite this shift of bias in the course of the story, gives a crowded picture of the last days of the French republic and shows young intellectuals finding hope by going to the working class: Denise Tessat, for example, is set in contrast to her brother Lucien, who goes from left wing to right. Altogether, *The Fall of Paris* is Ehrenburg's most impressive novel, notable for its picture of the decay of France between 1935 and 1940. After he finished it, Ehrenburg went as a correspondent to the Russian-German front, and his dispatches took a leading place all over the world among the battle reports of the time. Various other Russian authors wrote about the war from close observation, including Aleksei Tolstoy, who turned out an exciting series of stories he wrote in 1942 about a partisan he called Ivan Sudarev, who fought the invading Germans.

A short novel, *S frontovym privetom* (1945; *With Greetings from the Front*), by Valentin Ovechkin, is largely dialectic. Captain Spivak, who has been wounded, is at the beginning of the story in a railway car returning to the front. He listens to the people in the compartment discussing the war. After he rejoins his unit, he and his battalion commander, who is a fellow townsman, write a letter of hope to the people of their village, "with greetings from the front."

Mikhail Sholokhov's *Oni srazhalis' za rodinu* (*They Fought for Their Homeland*) was a war novel whose opening chapters came out in *Pravda* in 1943 and 1944; later the entire first part was published in 1955, with an announcement that the rest would follow sometime. Moscow's literary rumor is that in the early 1960s Sholokhov demanded from Khrushchev an early publication of the rest of this novel, but that Brezhnev prevented it, objecting to some anti-Stalinist parts of Sholokhov's text. The story is again about Cossacks at war, this time during their retreat across the Don, a hazardous operation involving great slaughter and injury, with damage to the collective farms of the region. This is one of the most impressive stories of the conflict.

Another combat novel set in the Don area, Valentin Katayev's *Syn polka* (1945; *The Son of a Regiment*), is the story of a boy, adopted by a combat regiment, who undergoes many exciting adventures. Alexander Fadeyev wrote of a group of young fighters in *Molodaya gvardiya* (*The Young Guard*), which first appeared in the magazine *Znamya* in 1945. Based on fact, it told the story of a group of Young Communist League members in the German-occupation zone, most of whom were executed. Soviet critics at first praised the novel for its picture of youthful heroism, but subsequently criticized it because it showed the ineptitude of older members of the Party in directing the regional underground. Later versions that appeared in 1947 and 1951 changed the story considerably and weakened it in the process, omitting the lively descriptions of the retreat and the beginning of the occupation. Yet Fadeyev himself was guilty of using his power in the Party to persecute other, more liberal writers. Khrushchev's revelations of the Stalinist atrocities frightened Fadeyev. He feared his own exposé as an oppressor. Feeling disgraced and threatened, Fadeyev lapsed into drunkenness and in 1956 killed himself.

Leonid Leonov, whose novels *The Thief* and *Soviet River* were mentioned earlier, wrote several wartime plays which will be considered later, and he also turned out a short novel, *Vzyatiye Velikoshumska* (1944; *The Taking of Velikoshumsk*, translated as *Chariot of Wrath*). In the framework of the story, a Soviet general makes an inspection tour of the front, but the principal action deals with a tank crew he encounters, four men expertly projected. In an attack, described at once forcefully and impressionistically, two of the soldiers meet their death. Another novel with an intimate picture of fighting men is Vasily Grossman's *Narod bessmerten* (1943; *People Are Immortal*), whose action takes place during the fierce German attacks on the Gomel sector of the Belorussian front. Patriotic rather than propagandistic, it is a fine picture of men at war, one of whom says that in fighting for his native land he has discovered it for the first time. In Boris Gorbatov's *Semya Tarasa* (1943; *Taras's Family*, also known as *Nepokoryonnyie, The Unvanquished*), the family of old Taras lives in a town of the Kuban region on the Germans' road to Stalingrad. Taras and his sons, who are virtually figures out of Gogol, take part in the opposition to the Nazis, either as soldiers or guerrillas; Taras's daughter, who also operates with the guerrillas, is captured and hanged by the Germans. The family seems to be symbolic of Russia itself as the victim of a devastating attack who strikes back courageously.

Besides the war novels, many short stories by Soviet writers dealt with the conflict. Aleksei Tolstoy's *Ivan Sudarev* tales have already been mentioned. The naval aspects of the war are the subject of Leonid Sobolev's collection of stories, *Morskaya dusha* (1942; *Soul of the Sea*), while Nikolai Tikhonov wrote a series of sketches of the siege of Leningrad in *Cherty sovetskogo cheloveka* (1943; *Characteristics of the Soviet Man*). None of this work was of the caliber of Isaac Babel's stories of the Red cavalry in the civil war.

It will be appropriate to close by discussing two more of the many novels about the war that appeared in Soviet Russia during these years: Viktor Nebrasov's *V okopakh Stalingrada* (1946; *In the Trenches at Stalingrad*) and Konstantin Simonov's *Dni i nochi* (1945; *Days and Nights*). These both deal with the Red Army in the most fateful and devastating battle and siege of the war. Nekrasov, who originally called *In the Trenches at Stalingrad* merely *Stalingrad*, was born in Paris in 1910, evidently the son of antitsarist Russians. His parents seem to have returned to Russia at the beginning of the First World War, and young Nekrasov studied to be an architect. His frontline service in the Second World War enabled him to give a participant's account of the war; the narrator in his novel is a young lieutenant. The author doesn't deal so much with actual combat as with the humdrum of military routine. Nekrasov's spokesman doesn't hesitate to point out mistakes made by the high command, and for this several Soviet critics attacked the book. Proud of his war service and the acclaim by his readers, Nekrasov was emboldened to criticism of the Party and even the KGB (*Komitet gosudarstvennoi bezopasnosti*, or Committee of State Security), in the postwar years. He was particularly frank and sharp about Soviet flaws in late 1962 when he published his impressions of travels in Italy and the United States. In the late sixties and early seventies he became a courageous dissident. In 1973–74, the Soviet secret police hounded him energetically, repeatedly searching his Kiev home and interrogating him harshly, on one occasion for six straight days. When he tried to escape the persecution by moving to Moscow, the police arrested him and deported him back to Kiev. His war service was no longer his shield.

Simonov, in *Days and Nights*, wrote from the point of view of a poet who had visited the front lines as a correspondent. He glorifies both the army and the higher command, and although his novel is somewhat spoiled by a conventional love story, it became the Soviet Union's most popular book of fiction about the war. It concerns the adventures of Captain Saburov, an average young man who becomes a battle hero; he has a somewhat awkward love affair with a nurse. Simonov, whose poetry will be discussed later, wrote another war novel between 1955 and 1959; *Zhivyie i myortvyie* (*The Living and the Dead*), dealing with a political commissar, of lieutenant's rank, named Vanya Sintsov, who experiences the horrors of the first phase of the war, when the Germans were overrunning Russia, with the Luftwaffe knocking Soviet bombers on the ground more often than out of the sky and the tanks moving forward inexorably. But Sintsov, who is once with a unit surrounded by the Nazis and breaks out of the encirclement, realizes by the end of the book, when he is a staff sergeant after a demotion, that the Russians will win, although a long war lies ahead of them.

2   Soviet Wartime Drama

During the war, when so many spontaneously patriotic plays appeared, nationalism was the theme. There were fewer cries against Formalism or in favor of Socialist realism, though these were to sound again after 1945. In the period of conflict numerous theaters had to close their doors as cities came under air attack and ground fire. Some of the Leningrad and Moscow acting companies removed to the Urals and other outlying places, but many also went to perform for troops at the front and set up theaters in the battle zones. At home, the playhouses that remained open did so under hazard and with great sacrifice; during the siege of Leningrad, for example, audiences wrapped in blankets and furs attended the classical and Soviet repertory.

Many of the plays of the time were hastily contrived to fit events of the moment, but a few good dramas were written, especially by the novelist Leonid Leonov, some of whose plays have been previously mentioned, also by Alexander Korneychuk, Konstantin Simonov, Alexander Gladkov, Nikolai Pogodin, and others. The latter include the pairs of collaborators, Mikhail Vodopyanov-Yuri Laptev and M. Shtitelman-Grigory Kats.

These writing teams turned out comedies in the war years. Shtitelman and Kats wrote *Tvoy dobryi drug* (1942; *Your Good Friend*), and Vodopyanov and Laptev wrote *Vynuzhdennaya posadka* (1943; *Forced Landing*). The former is somewhat of a throwback to the long-neglected comedy of manners: *Your Good Friend* is only by implication a war play, since it deals for the most part with secondary-school education. A young teacher named Netsvetai comes to a school in the south, where the townspeople, caricatures of stuffy bureaucrats, consider him arrogant, particularly after he scolds the head of the local soviet for not having brought his son up properly. Local officials plan to get rid of Netsvetai until word comes through that the people whom he had formerly served so well have arranged for him to receive government honors. Now those who had been trying to oust him suddenly appreciate him and encourage him to remain, but he feels that he must carry on his work elsewhere and so goes to an outpost in Northeastern Siberia. The dramatists have subtly suggested that Netsvetai is the kind of alert trainer of youth needed in wartime; the students in whom he had instilled his ideas have become war heroes, praised on the radio.

The comedy *Forced Landing* is about an air-force captain whose plane makes an emergency landing on a collective farm in an area retaken from the Germans. In the fashion of Shakespearean comedy, the young mechanic who repairs the plane is a girl in disguise, not recognized as such by the captain. Later the girl writes to explain her true identity, and the captain comes back to see her. The members of the community encourage the pair to marry and express the hope that they will settle on the collective, the bride driving a tractor, the groom wielding a scythe.

Still another comedy of the time had a historic setting: *Davnym davno* (1941; *Long, Long Ago*), by Alexander Gladkov (author of the novel *Cement*), takes place at the time of the Napoleonic wars. This "heroic comedy in verse," first performed in Leningrad when the city was under attack, has its share of calamities but an optimistic spirit dominates the play, which celebrates the heroism of the guerrillas of that earlier period. The French are rather grotesquely caricatured as Fascist-like villains.

As in Germany, historical plays were popular in Russia during the war. Aleksei Tolstoy at this time wrote the two parts of his *Ivan Groznyi* (*Ivan the Terrible*): *Oryol i orlitsa* (1942; *The Eagle and His Mate*), dealing with the years 1553–69, and *Trudnyie gody* (1943; *The Hard Years*), concentrating on the 1566–71 period. In these plays, Aleksei Tolstoy attempts to soften some of the previously harsh portraits of Ivan as a cruel tyrant. Another effort to make Ivan look better than historians of the past had made him out is Vladimir Solovyov's drama, *Velikiy gosudar'* (1945; *The Great Ruler*), which won the Stalin Prize, as his earlier historical play, *Feld'marshal Kutuzov* (*Field Marshal Kutuzov*) had won it in 1940. Interest in a tsarist general of the First World War who subsequently encouraged the Bolshevik armies to move against Poland in 1920 was manifested in several novels already mentioned, and in Ilya Selvinsky's drama, *General Brusilov* (1943). As for Aleksei Tolstoy's *Ivan the Terrible* dramas, they were not of the same quality as his novels, written in the same period, about Peter the Great.

One of the wartime plays of Nikolai Pogodin has been mentioned: *Kremlyovskiye kuranty* (1941; *The Kremlin Chimes*), it will be remembered, was partly about an old Jewish watchmaker who wanted the bells of the Kremlin to play the "Internationale." In *Lodochnitsa* (1943; *The Boat-*

woman), Pogodin celebrated the courage of the Russian women who kept the ferry running across the Volga at the time the Germans were besieging Stalingrad. *Sotvoreniye mira* (1945; *The Creation of the World*) concerned the construction of a new city out of the ruins the Nazis had left of the former city.

Konstantin Simonov didn't come up to the level of his novels with his play *Russkie lyudi* (1942; *The Russian People*), although it contains several interesting characters. Set in the south, it deals with the bravery of ordinary Soviet citizens in an area taken over by the Germans. A play filled with tense drama, *The Russian People* also contained many fine moments of comedy which delighted its audiences.

The opening scene showed the occupation-zone town at night, crackling with fires, the boots of German troops sounding amid cries and shots, all against the background of Shostakovich's *Seventh Symphony*. *The Russian People* won the second rather than the first Stalin Prize (Leonov's *Invasion* took the first prize in 1942), but Simonov's play proved to be an international success, produced in the United States by the Theatre Guild. This American success, however, didn't prevent Simonov from writing, in 1946, a vigorously anti-American play, *Russkiy vopros* (*The Russian Question*).

A highly topical and popular play, *Front* (1942; *The Front*), came from the pen of the Ukrainian author, Alexander Korneychuk. This treated a problem that was acute and often discussed during the war: how up-to-date were the military commanders who had served in the First World War and in the Russian civil war? In actuality, such old marshals as Voroshilov and Budyonny had to be replaced; Korneychuk's play, which to the surprise of many was allowed to appear (it came out first in *Pravda*), pointed up this problem. As presented at the Vakhtangov State Academic Drama Theater, and elsewhere throughout Russia, *The Front* was staged boldly, as an argument presented rather vehemently to its audiences. The Moscow Art Theater produced it with realistic restraint, with fine settings of forest and snowy landscape. In the drama, a former civil-war leader named Ivan Gorlov refuses to admit new ideas or, since he keeps old comrades as subordinates, new men. A young major general opposes Gorlov who, after a battle of ideas, is relieved from command.

Of all the Soviet war plays, the best are those of the novelist Leonid Leonov: *Nashestviye* (1941–42; *Invasion*) and *Lyonushka* (1942–43). Each of them won the Stalin Prize in the year of its appearance. *Invasion* is set in a small town which the Germans take and then lose. A man who has killed the woman he loved, and has then served in prison and a concentration camp, returns home to find that his father, a local doctor, will not leave the town despite the approach of the Germans. The doctor's son, Fyodor, offers his services to the regional partisan (guerrilla) group, who reject him. But after the Germans move in, Fyodor carries on his own war of terror against them, killing soldiers and officers and letting the partisans have the credit for his deeds in the eyes of the townspeople. The Germans arrest him and execute him just before the Russians recapture the town. Fyodor's mother says proudly of her son, "Finally he has become one of us!" The play, despite the Nazi stereotypes, is full of fine dramatic touches, and Fyodor's parents are skillfully characterized. The change in Fyodor, from a convict outcast to virtually a tragic hero, reveals Leonov's dramatic skill.

Leonov turned to the partisans again for *Lyonushka*, the story of a Ukrainian peasant girl of that name who had joined a guerrilla band. In their camp she nurses a wounded Soviet officer with whom she is in love; when he dies in spite of her efforts to save him, she goes with her fellow partisans to renew the attack on the invaders. A play that avoids rhetoric, *Lyonushka* is essentially nonrealistic, partly symbolic, a point which made some producers wary of presenting it lest they be accused of Formalism; but, as noted, it won the Stalin Prize and received acclaim as a forcefully patriotic play.

What the Soviet dramatists were mostly trying to convey was that their native land, their way of life, was worth fighting for, and that there would be a good life when peace arrived. This is the keynote of an important speech in Viktor

Gusev's "film scenario in verse," *V shest' chasov vechera posle voiny* (1943; *At Six O'Clock in the Evening after the War*), in which one of the characters says:

> And here I look at Moscow, my love,
> And I am full of joy to meet with her,
> And maybe I won't be able to find words,
> But that's not important, my friends.
> What's important is that we as a friendly family
> Shall go throughout our native land.
> We'll dry tears and heal wounds,
> We'll build palaces for children.

3   Soviet Wartime Poetry

Most of the poets of the epoch wrote on themes of war, the fatherland, and patriotism—even Boris Pasternak, who will be looked at in another chapter, wrote some war verses, though official critics found fault with them. Yet the amount of Soviet poetry worth talking about that came out of the war is not large.

One of the poetic achievements of the time was *Vasily Tyorkin*, a semihumorous long poem about a soldier. Its author was Alexander Tvardovsky (1910–71), who had earlier, in 1930, written a book of verse celebrating the collective farms *Put' k sotsializmu* (*The Road to Socialism*) and, in 1936, a long poem *Strana Muraviya* (*The Land of Muravia*) which won a Stalin Prize. It is the story of a young peasant who refuses to join the *kolkhoz* and wanders about seeking the imaginary land of Muravia, a paradise beyond his grasp; he ends by joining the collective. The poem is full of folklore and peasant idiom, with shrewd character sketches of various types. Aside from its obvious bow to the imperatives of Soviet censorship, the poem exists in its own right. So does Tvardovsky's epic of the Russian soldier at war.

Vasily Tyorkin treats of the disasters of battle but also of its humorous side. Vasily himself is named for a character created by a pre-Soviet writer, Pyotr Boborykin, whose Vasily

Tyorkin was really a rogue. In Tvardovsky's hands he becomes the good-humored GI Joe of the Red Army, and rather than being roguish he is merely ingenious, as well as often ingenuous. The poem appeared serially during the war and was extremely popular. By the time Berlin was taken, however, the official critics and censors wanted writers to start praising the fresh, new life that was beginning, so Vasily Tyorkin's adventures came to an end. But Tvardovsky permitted himself one last indulgence in the final part of the poem, when he wrote of the grief of the soldier who had lost his entire family during the war. Tvardovsky wrote that he hoped the experiences he had related would be remembered in the future, after several drinks of beer, by the veteran with the empty sleeve.

One of the most prolific of the war poets, Aleksei Surkov (born in 1899), has written some thirty volumes of poems, including his *Izbrannyie stikhi* (1936, 1947; *Selected Poems*). Surkov, who has always been an extremist in advocating the Party-line doctrine—his political career will be dealt with later—had before the Second World War written vigorously about the civil war in verses filled with implacable hatred of the enemy, and he had produced chauvinistic poems about the Red Army's marching triumphantly into Europe in the future. As a war poet, he seemed a different man: in his verse he grieved over the destruction caused by the German advance, he patriotically exhorted his countrymen to fight back, and he wrote mellow poems about comradeship at the front. His war songs were sung everywhere, in trenches, on farms, and in cities. On the day of the German invasion, Surkov wrote his famous song, "Pesnya smelykh" ("The Song of the Bold Ones"), and later the highly popular "Pesnya zashchitnikov Moskvy" ("Song of the Defenders of Moscow"). Some of his poems of the time were evocations of Russia's great past, as in "Rodina" ("My Country"); but now and then a hatred of the opposing army was expressed, as it had been in some of Surkov's civil-war poems. This last note is particularly noticeable in his book *Dekabr' pod Moskvoi* (1942; *December before Moscow*). It would of course be difficult to expect the Soviet people not to hate the

Nazis who had invaded their land and begun devastating it; but the poetry of nostalgia and glorification seems to have been as common as verse of hatred.

One of the remarkable poems of the war was by the novelist and playwright, Konstantin Simonov: "Ty pomnish', Alyosha, dorogi Smolenshchiny" ("You Remember, Alyosha, the Roads of Smolensk"). The Alyosha of the poem is Alexander Surkov, to whom Simonov says that his homeland seems now to be not the house in the city where he had spent happy times, but rather the soil known by their grandfathers, who are now buried in graves under plain crosses. He invokes those grandfathers as he goes along the roads the Russian armies took during their early retreats: these ancestral figures should pray for their sons who were unbelievers (a section of the poem not reprinted in some of the later editions). The poet feels proud to be a Russian, proud to have had a Russian mother.

Simonov's short lyric, "Zhdi menya" ("Wait for Me"), was even more popular, the yearning of a soldier at the front for the woman he loves. And the poetry of love is predominant in Simonov's volume *S toboi i bez tebya* (1944; *With You and without You*), which some Party-line critics found fault with as being too individualistic. Simonov is a popular poet, but not first-rate; his plays, which can be sentimental as the poems are, also have tendential qualities; his finest work remains his novels.

A good deal of the Soviet wartime verse dealt with the besieged cities, and with the heroism shown by the soldiers defending them and by the civilian population. In 1956 the woman poet Yuliya Neyman could in her "1941" evoke the days and nights of courage shown by the people of Moscow amid blackouts and calamities, so that the poet was proud to share citizenship with them. At the time, various poems were also written about Leningrad, which withstood the German onslaughts.

The former Acmeist, Nikolai Tikhonov, wrote about the besieged city of the north in *Leningradskiye rasskazy* (1942; *Leningrad Tales*) and in his long poem, *Kirov s nami* (1942; *Kirov Is with Us*). The latter, which won a Stalin Prize,

conjured up the spirit of Sergei M. Kirov, the popular secretary of the Party in Leningrad whose murder late in 1934
had led to the famous conspiracy trials known as the purges.
Historians have come to suspect strongly that Stalin himself
had ordered the death of his friend Kirov, who was a moderate; if Stalin had anything to do with the murder, as it now
seems quite likely, the awarding of a prize in his name for a
poem devoted to Kirov is a supreme irony. Tikhonov shows
Kirov going around the besieged city on a black and icy night.

Vera Inber won a Stalin Prize for her long poem, *Pul-
kovskiy meridian* (1943; *The Pulkovo Meridian*), a picture
of life in the besieged city. She became increasingly slavish
to Party slogans. Between the war and her death in 1972 she
did not equal her wartime verses.

Leningrad, which was encircled by the Germans in September 1941, was cut off from the world until the following
February, when food once more began to come into the city,
this time across the ice of Lake Lagoda, "the road of life."
During the winter, about six hundred thousand people in
Leningrad died. The miseries of the blockade and the resistance of the people were indeed stirring themes for poetry,
as the work of three other women poets—Olga Bergholz,
Margarita Aligher, and Anna Akhmatova—shows.

Olga Bergholz, born in 1910, broadcast on the Leningrad
radio as long as it operated; she put her poems together in
Leningradskaya tetrad' (1942; *The Leningrad Notebook*), a
series of clear and detailed pictures of the siege. But she was
also remembered for the powerful, heartrending poems she
wrote about the misery caused her, not alone by the Nazis,
but by the Soviet secret police who arrested her husband
shortly before the war. Still she wanted to believe in his
survival and eventual return home—as if to speed this happiness in coming, she always set a waiting plate for him op-
posite her as she sat down to her scanty meals.

Margarita Aligher, born in 1915, wrote in "Moya pobeda"
("My Victory") of a woman's personal response to the war,
while in "Zoya" she told the story of the girl, Zoya, who was
tortured and killed by the Germans. She also wrote a long
poem about the siege, part of which is "Vesna v Leningrade"
(1942; "Spring in Leningrad").

In the course of the slow winter,
Breaking the iron darkness—
"We will not yield. We are stone"—
You would say in a quiet voice.
Always the poisonous ring drawing around us.
The enemy keeps coming closer.
Finally the people of Leningrad
Stared, as soldiers,
Into his sullen face.
O city of no light or water!
The siege rations of 125 grammes of bread . . .

From the merciless, dead sky
A bestial growl of trouble.
The stones groaned,
                    the pavements gasped,
While people found strength to live,
And those who died went like warriors
Into shared and crowded graves.

But at last winter grew weary,
The troubled distances opened,
And the bombed houses stood up black—
They were dead, they had yielded.
And you and I together walk onto the bridges,
And under the wing of triumphant May
You are stirred up and joyous,
Without knowing the reason for this.
And you and I together look at a cloud,
As the breeze makes our eyes and lips cold.
And together we quietly speak of past and future.
Both of us have battled out of the long darkness
And gone through barrages of flame.
You used to say, "We are stone."
No,
      we are stronger than stone,
                              we—live.

It remained for that older superb poet, Anna Akhmatova,
to write about the war with the deepest feeling and most
chiseled style. In "Muzhevsto" ("Courage"), Akhmatova

created one of the truly great Russian war poems. It says in part:

> *Dying of a bullet is nothing to fear,*
> *And finding yourself roofless is not unbearable;*
> *Everything is endured, O great language we love:*
> *You, Russian tongue, are what must be saved,*
>   *and we vow*
> *We will give you in purity to the sons of our sons.*

In time international fame came to her most deservedly. As Richard Wilbur wrote: "The voice of Akhmatova . . . is both passionate and finished, both reckless and austere." Stanley Kunitz paid his homage: "Tragedy did not wither her: it crowned her with majesty."

But Stalin and his associates thought they knew better. They wanted no true and profound feeling and beauty in the arts, nor any experimentation. The postwar reaction increased the whip's velocity. From 1945 to his death in 1948 Andrei Zhdanov, that high henchman of Stalin, the sub-dictator of literature, music, and other arts, let loose an especially ferocious drive against nonconformity in the arts, with personal attacks on the poetess Anna Akhmatova and, as already stated, on the humorist Mikhail Zoshchenko, practically forbidding them to write and publish. Akhmatova in particular was singled out for repression, and, as already mentioned, even her young son Lev Gumilyov, a talented archeologist-writer, was placed under arrest and exiled for a time.

6

Stalin's Death and the Time of Thaw

Stalin died in March 1953, yet the change for the better didn't come during that momentous year but one year later. It was in 1954 that a few Soviet writers began to extol human needs, human love, and the virtues of the family as above those of the Party and the state, the rights of the individual over the demands of the Plan, of industrialization and collectivization.

The first book off the presses was Ehrenburg's novel *Ottepel'* (1954–56; *The Thaw*), a title which gave the name to the entire immediate post-Stalin period in Soviet life as well as literature. Then came Vladimir Dudintsev's *Ne khlebom yedinym* (1957; *Not by Bread Alone*); Galina Nikolayeva's *Bitva v puti* (1957; *A Battle En Route*); Konstantin Paustovsky's contemplative stories and relaxed memoirs, and other paeans to human values.

With every such novel and story, increasingly the villains were not the old-style "unrepentant" intellectuals who could not adjust to Soviet heroics; not the assorted cardboard characters of wreckers, spies, and other hidden, slimy agents of foreign capitalism. Now, for a breathtaking change, the villains were the soulless, cruel, Stalin-elevated bureaucrats; heads of Soviet factories, driving themselves and hordes of their subordinate engineers and workers to fulfill the Plan. These captains of Soviet industries were depicted as a hard-hearted caste who had built this vast prison instead of the promised Socialist paradise, in the process—almost incidentally, yet significantly—neglecting and even mistreating their own wives and families, depriving them of tender love and compassion.

Tvardovsky was allowed a fuller measure of his liberalism when, through Khrushchev's personal order, the poet's moving *Za dal'yu—dal'* (*Distance after Distance*), begun in 1950, was finally permitted publication ten years later and given the Lenin Prize in 1961. Significantly, as editor of the influential monthly *Novy mir* (*New World*), Tvardovsky sought out, published, and encouraged new writers to express themselves fearlessly in both substance and style.

From the middle 1950s on, not alone *Novy mir*, but also *Yunost'* (*Youth*), and a few other monthly magazines and annual almanacs dared to publish frank fiction, bold poems, challenging essays, unorthodox reviews, with newly ringing proclamations of experiment and demands for creative and even political freedom. For once, although too briefly, the old dogmatist Stalinists seemed to be on the defensive or shamed into a silence.

This post-Stalinist relaxation brought with it rehabilitation of at least a few formerly repressed writers. For some it was, alas, posthumous only. But others were still alive, notably Anna Akhmatova. Following Stalin's death, she was honored and almost revered, although in her old age she now wrote little that was epoch-making. Yet her past glory was now reaffirmed. In 1962 an official Soviet announcement proclaimed: "Akhmatova is a great master of verse form—classically transparent, finely sharpened, complete."

Mikhail Bulgakov did not of course live to see the latter-day resurrection of his work. Soon after his death in 1940, two of his plays had been staged (1941 and 1943), but none of his fiction was reprinted until 1955. Small editions of it were permitted by Khrushchev's government, for some ten years. Then, in 1965, with a spectacular rush, Bulgakov's name and work were made prominent, gaining reborn recognition both at home and in the West. His *Teatral'nyi roman* (*The Theatrical Novel*) appeared in 1965, and, most impressively, *Master i Margarita* (*The Master and Margarita*) was published in 1966–67, first as a magazine serial, then as a book, this last mainly in Western Europe. In late 1973, unexpectedly, with no prior announcement, the Artistic Literature Publishing House in Moscow brought out a one-volume collection of Bulgakov's works, including the Turbin opus, *The Theatrical Novel*, and *The Master and Margarita*. Its edition of 30,000 copies was immediately bought up in the bookstores by eager readers at the official price of 1 ruble 53 kopeks (rated as $2.03), and soon, in January 1974, the black-market price was fifty rubles (almost $67) per copy.

While *Teatral'nyi roman* lampooned Stanislavsky and the Moscow Art Theater, attacking the excessive worship paid that hallowed institution, *The Master and Margarita* was far more profound and even mystic, proclaiming as it did that man as a spiritual entity is an enigma, apparently not at all yielding to a facile key provided by Marxism. The new Soviet reader, barred by the Party from any indulgence in mysticism and metaphysics, hankered after Bulgakov's novel; its scarce editions are much sought after on Russia's literary black market.

Some of Bulgakov's writings, hidden in his desk drawers in his lifetime, were not allowed even a magazine publication in the easier post-Stalin times. Thus his novelette *Sobachye serdtse* (*The Dog's Heart*) was not permitted in the Soviet Union, and had to be published in the West. So intimidated was Bulgakov's widow that on a visit in France she was shocked to see this story's galley proofs in a Paris printery. She hesitated about its eventual publication, but the Russian émigrés in charge of the project went ahead anyway. This tale, as well as Bulgakov's early story "Rokovyie yaitsa" ("The Fatal Eggs"), acidly questions the viability of a Socialist-Communist society. Both show a grotesque miscarriage of Soviet experimentation: a dog becomes an ugly tyrant over man; some eggs, treated by a wondrous ray, hatch not giant chickens but monstrous reptiles.

New young talents appeared in the period of Thaw in both Soviet prose and Soviet poetry. Let us begin with the discussion of three men named Yuri.

Yuri Nagibin (born in 1920 in Moscow) fought in the war in 1941–43 and continued as a war correspondent until 1945. He was graduated from the Institute of Cinematography, but his first story "Dvoinaya oshibka" ("The Double Mistake") had already appeared in 1939. His first collection of tales *Chelovek s fronta* (*The Man from the Front*) came out in 1943. This was followed by a prolific output of stories, novellas, and novels, of which his frankly autobiographical *Pavlik* (1959; *Little Paul*) is among the best. The post-Stalinist reader liked Nagibin's striving for man's inner purity, his proclamation of the need for beauty and honesty in human relations.

Yuri Bondaryov (born in 1924 in the southern Urals) fought in the Second World War as an artillery officer and began to write in 1949. After a number of short stories and several novels devoted to the war in a patriotic yet sensitive vein, which quickly found a wide readership, he wrote the novel *Tishina* (1962; *Stillness*), which was clearly anti-Stalinist and otherwise nonconformist, drawing much attention and a young following, although some official Party frowns, too. Regretfully, as if in fear and trembling for his career, Bondaryov in January 1974 came out with a public attack on Solzhenitsyn for his antipurge book *Arkhipelag GULag* (*The Gulag Archipelago*) which we will discuss in our later pages.

Yuri Kazakov (born in 1927), the son of a Moscow worker, was early interested in music, beginning its study in 1944 and playing in both jazz and classical orchestras until 1963. But already in 1953 he turned to literature. Entering the Gorky Literary Institute, he was graduated from it in 1958. His first stories were published in magazines in 1956; it is from this year on that he now considers his beginnings as a professional writer.

His collection of short stories *Na polustanke* (1959; *At a Small Railroad Station*) drew an immediate attention of critics and an admiration of readers. His sense of lyricism, his subtle yet realistic portrayal of deeply personal experiences, won him a large and ever growing public. Kazakov traveled a great deal, particularly in the Russian Far North, whence he brought to his appreciative readers his rare understanding of nature. His subsequent books of stories were *Severnyi dnevnik* (1961; *Northern Diary*); *Goluboye i zelyonoye* (1963; *Azure-Blue and Green*); and *Dvoye v dekabre* (1966; *Two in December*). In English one of the best collections of Kazakov's work is *Going to Town and Other Stories,* compiled and translated by the late Gabriella Azrael (Boston, 1964).

A yet younger arrival was Vasily Aksyonov (born in 1932 in Kazan). He lost his father, a high Communist official, in the Stalinist purges. His mother Yevgeniya Ginzburg survived long years of prisons and other appalling persecution (she wrote her reminiscences in the book *Krutoi marshrut,* or *The Steep Route,* banned in the Soviet Union but published in the West in 1967 both in Russian and, among other languages, in English as *Journey into the Whirlwind*). The son Vasily was taken to a state children's home. He grew up to graduate from a medical school but became a writer in 1959, with his stories about the rebellious Soviet youth arousing both popularity and controversy. He wrote the novelette *Kolleghi* (1960; *Colleagues*) about young Soviet physicians; the novel *Zvyozdnyi bilet* (1961; *A Ticket to the Stars*); also *Na polputi k lune* (1962; *Halfway to the Moon*); *Apel'siny iz Marokko* (1963; *Oranges from Morocco*). For a time he was in the vanguard of the liberating movement in Soviet literature as one of the editors of the *Yunost'* magazine. In the early 1970s he and a collaborator wrote a spoof of James Bond's adventures, creating "Gene Green Untouchable: CIA Agent 014," which nonetheless was taken seriously by Soviet readers who by 1973 bought 100,000 copies of the parody—and by Yevgeny Yevtushenko who publicly and vigorously attacked the spoof as "a harmful production."

Anatoly Kuznetsov, eventually causing a worldwide sensation by defecting to the West, was born in 1931 and as a boy lived in Nazi-occupied Kiev at the time of the wholesale massacre of Jews in the huge ravine called Babiy Yar. Kuznetsov became famous in the 1950s and '60s by writing about the massacre in his book *Babiy Yar,* as also about young people's pioneering in Siberia in his *Prodolzheniye leghendy* (English version in 1959, *Sequel to a Legend, from the Diary of a Young Man*). On his defection in London in July 1969,

Kuznetsov charged that Soviet editors and censors had grossly distorted his texts. From then on he busied himself publishing in the West the undistorted originals of his books.

In Khrushchev's time the Soviet censors and distorters operated in fits and starts, now permitting a limited amount of candor and criticism, not smiting the daring writers in nearly a fury. At certain times in the period of Thaw and well into the early 1960s, the wretched life on Soviet collective farms was permitted as the subject for writers, and so came a number of frank accounts by several talented authors. In this new and behind-the-scenes *kolkhoz* literature, Fyodor Abramov drew instant recognition with his hard-hitting *Vokrug i okolo* (1963; *Around and About*; published in English, also in 1963, as *One Day in the "New Life"*). There was also Alexander Yashin (1913–68, real name Popov), with his short stories "Rychaghi" (1956; "Levers") and "Vologodskaya svad'ba" (1962; "The Vologda Wedding"); and Vladimir Tendryakov (born in 1923), with his novella *Konchina* (1968; *Death*). In the same *kolkhoz* genre the story "Matryonin dvor" (1963; "Matryona's Yard") by Alexander Solzhenitsyn (of whom much more in our later chapters) was one of the few allowed to be published in the Soviet Union before a complete ban was placed on this great writer's works by the Soviet rulers.

A kind of penance for his servility in Stalin's time may be seen in such latter-day works by an old Soviet master of fiction as Valentin Katayev's two novels, *Svyatoi kolodets* (1967; *The Holy Well*) and *Trava zabveniya* (1967; *Grass of Oblivion*), both books a far cry from the straitjacket of Socialist realism. In the same category of repentance by an old writer there seems to be Leonid Leonov's novel *Evgenia Ivanovna*, a story about a sympathetically drawn Russian émigré lady (now married to an English gentleman) who returns home after many years for a visit and meets her former Russian husband, the latter presented not at all positively. This novel was published in 1963, and Leonov took care to explain that it was originally written in 1938 but had to be confined to his desk, since its appearance in those Stalinist days would have been unthinkable.

Some of the old-time Soviet poets tried to pick up the later-day liberal tune but their sincerity was in doubt and their courage did not last. Pavel Antokolsky, born in 1896 in St. Petersburg in a lawyer's family, began to publish in 1921 and his first book of poems came out in 1922. His early notable books of verse, *Zapad* (1926; *The West*) and *Tretya kniga* (1927; *The Third Book*), were romantic in themes and tones, yet cautiously loyal to the Soviet régime. During the Second World War his poems were patriotic as well as lyrical. He joined the Communist Party in 1943. In the later 1950s he attempted to speak in praise of freedom; his book of verse *Masterskaya* (1957; *The Workshop*) appeared to be among such efforts. But the Party line prevailed in his book of prose and poetry *Sila Vietnama* (1960; *Vietnam's Strength*).

Another survivor of the Stalinist times was Alexander Prokofyev, born in 1900, the son of a peasant-fisherman, who fought in the civil war on the Red side, and whose best books of poetry were *Doroga cherez most* (1933; *The Road across the Bridge*) and *Pryamyie stikhi* (1936; *Straight Verses*). He achieved renown in 1944 with his wartime poem *Rossiya* (*Russia*), winning the Stalin Prize in 1946. In post-Stalinist times his books included *Yablonya nad morem* (1958; *The Apple Tree over the Sea*) and *Stikhi s dorogi* (1963; *Verses En Route*). His erstwhile merry experimentation with the Russian language, which was an influence over him by the freer poets of the early 1920s, gave way to his strict laconic quality of thirty and forty years later.

Nikolai Zabolotsky (1903–58), whose fine poetry in its spirit, style, and form was close to those of Western masters, and who was arrested by the secret police as early as the 1920s, boldly warned his fellow literati and other intellectuals in the freer 1950s that the Thaw would not last. He died before he could see his own prophecy come true.

Mixed trends are evident in the work of a number of Soviet writers who now proclaim the beauty and necessity of human freedom, but who lie low as the very latest resurgence of censorship threatens them. Independence of various kinds in sundry times has been shown by such authors as Granin and Soloukhin.

Daniil Granin (real name Daniil Gherman, born in 1918 in the Kursk Province) was an electrical engineer until the Second World War and a tank squadron commander at the front. He began to write in the late 1940s. In 1957 his story "Sobstvennoye mneniye" ("Personal Opinion") was officially criticized as too nonconformist. Of his prolific creative output the novel *Idu na grozu* (1963; *I Go Out into the Storm*), showing a new independence of Soviet scientists and engineers, is best known.

A singular proponent of resurrecting old cultural values of tsarist times (including the restoration of ancient churches and ikons) appeared in the person of Vladimir Soloukhin (born in 1924 in the Central Russian region of Vladimir) whose stories, verse, and essays show a lively talent and a curious respect for Russia's past but whose public activities show loyalty and near-servility to the Party line.

Science fiction, which has had its practitioners and public for many decades in Russia (although not too artistically and, except for a few stories, has remained untranslated into Western language), has recently come to the fore thanks to the remarkable writings of the two Strugatsky brothers, Arkady and Boris, working as a team. While Arkady (born in 1925 in Batumi) by profession and livelihood is an astronomer, Boris (born in 1933 in Leningrad) is a linguist specializing in the Japanese language. In 1957 they began to write their "social fantasy"—the utopias and the antiutopias. Most of their work remains in magazines, but a book of novellas *Vozvrashcheniye* (*Return*) did finally appear in 1962. Other novellas and novels, mostly to be found in periodicals and almanacs, are: *Trudno byt' bogom* (1964; *It's Hard To Be a God*); *Khishchnyie veshchi veka* (1965; *Rapacious Things of the Age*); *Ulitka na sklone* (1966–68; *The Snail on the Slope*); *Vtoroye nashestviye marsian* (1967; *The Second Invasion of Martians*); *Obitayemyi ostrov* (1969; *The Inhabited Island*); and *Malysh* (1971; *The Youngster*).

Despite its appearance mostly in obscure, regional (Siberian and other), small-circulation journals, the two brothers' work has by these middle 1970s achieved a tremendous popularity among both the masses and the intellectuals all over the Soviet Union. The two authors lay their scenes and action in a vague West of tomorrow, but the readers know that the locale is none other but their own Russia of today. Political heresy—satire aimed at the Communist system—cannot be mistaken. Those novels, novelettes, and stories are copied by readers from the obscure magazines in thousands of pages, which are then handed or mailed from friend to friend or black-marketed from seller to client in all parts of the Soviet Union.

Official critics attack the brothers Strugatsky for their daring nonconformism; the regional editors in Siberia and elsewhere are denounced for printing such bold and clever dissent; but the onslaught only whets the appetite of the readers for the Strugatsky creations. And somehow, despite all the official Soviet thunder against them, the brothers continue to write and be printed. For, it is said, they do have some powerful protectors in the inner sanctums of the Soviet Establishment.

On the other hand, in the mid-1950s and certainly by the end of that decade, a few writers and editors emerged on the Soviet scene who protested against liberalization. Leading among such dogmatists and neo-Stalinists was Vsevolod Kochetov (1912–73), who as the editor of the monthly magazine *Oktyabr'* and a fictioneer in his own right proclaimed the need for a return to Stalinism. His novel *Bratya Yershovy* (1958; *The Yershov Brothers*) was meant as an indignant answer to Dudintsev's indictment of bureaucrats. Kochetov followed it with *Zhurbiny* (1960; *The Zhurbins*) and *Sekretar' obkoma* (1961; *Secretary of the Regional Committee*), each of these novels a hymn to conformity.

Following the Hungarian revolt of 1956 and through 1962 Khrushchev himself articulated his second thoughts about the permissiveness in the arts and in other means of expression he had initiated in his reforms. He ordered screws to be applied, even if gradually. On one occasion, reading a riot act to a group of summoned writers and artists, he actually threatened them with shooting, whereupon (it is said) at least one of the guests, the sensitive poetess Margarita Aligher, promptly fainted. Under Khrushchev's successors Kochetov became even more vicious in his writings. His novel *Chego zhe ty khochesh'?* (1969; *What Then Do You Want?*) was a particularly bitter attack on the Soviet liberal intelligentsia.

Since the mid-1950s original and rebellious voices of several young Soviet poets have been raised significantly. Yet, the most publicized of these has proved to be a disappointment. This is Yevgeny Yevtushenko (born in Siberia in 1933), whose poems "Stantsiya Zima" ("The Station Winter"), "The Babiy Yar" (about the large-scale massacre of Jews by the Nazis at that place on Kiev's fringe), "Nasledniki Stalina" ("Stalin's Heirs") at first sounded like a true trumpet call to freedom but in time were diminished in their force by much of the poet's other, far more opportunistic verses. By the late 1960s and early '70s Yevtushenko seemed to be a servitor of the Communist Establishment, rewarded by the rulers with frequent and luxurious journeys to foreign lands; but after Alexander Solzhenitsyn's banishment in 1974, Yevtushenko caused trouble for himself by making protests against that ugly event.

A finer poet and a more genuine rebel, Andrei Voznesensky (born in 1933 in Moscow), produces work deeper in form and content, at times quite obscure. His outstanding long poem "Oza" (a woman's name contrived by the poet), has been a favorite among Soviet scientists and other intellectuals since its first appearance in the magazine *Molodaya gvardiya* in October 1964. Voznesensky pretends that his poem is a notebook found on a night table in a hotel room at Dubna, the Soviet atomic research center. He sings of his scientist friends whom he calls "the gods"; of the woman who stands by a cyclotron and "listens, fully magnetized." He fuses mechanization with mysticism, laboratory with love, and protest with poetry.

Two years earlier, in 1962, on a visit in Paris, Voznesensky was asked: "Your poetry is not easy to understand at first sight, yet you are published in editions of 50,000 to 120,000 copies. Who are your readers?"

Voznesensky replied, "The people who especially like modern poetry are the young physicists, the young scientists,

men who, while they appear very uncomplicated and ordinary, do complex things and are complex people. Thus
they don't want overly simple poetry, just as they are not
interested in primitive tools."

At least in part Voznesensky's interest in modern technological themes is explained by the fact of his scientific-
technical background: his father was a scientist, and the poet
himself was graduated from a school of architecture.

The new poets of the 1950s, '60s, and '70s also include the
fresh and sometimes nonconformist voices of Boris Slutsky
(born in 1919 in the Ukraine) and Robert Rozhdestvensky
(born in 1932). But there is an interesting difference between these two: while Slutsky seldom, if at all, bends before
the hectoring of the Party and the government, Rozhdestvensky does now and then change his tune, becoming "anti-
imperialist" on occasion to suit the new tightening of the
Communist lid on poetic expression in the Soviet Union of
these Brezhnev-Kosygin times.

An unusually popular poet Bulat Okudzhava, author of
poems and ballads (and, more recently, fiction), was born
in 1924 in Moscow, the son of a Georgian father and an
Armenian mother. His father, a zealous Communist, died
in the Stalinist purges. Bulat volunteered as a Red Army
combatant, returning from the Second World War with
wounds and decorations—and as a confirmed pacifist. He
began to publish in 1953, his poems in *Yunost'*, *Molodaya
gvardiya*, and other journals drawing enthusiastic attention,
particularly among young readers. His resounding fame came
from his own performance of his antibureaucracy, anti-
Stalinist, and pacifist ballads on the stage to the accompaniment of his guitar. The post-Stalin Soviet government tried
to stop him; it threatened him with punishment; but eager
listeners made hundreds of tapes of his performances, and
the Soviet rulers seemed helpless in their attempts to halt
him and his ever growing audience.

Okudzhava's first book of poems *Lirika* (1956; *Lyrics*) was
followed by *Ostrova* (1959; *Islands*); *Vesyolyi barabanshchik*
(1964; *The Merry Drummer*); and *Mart velikodushnyi*
(1967; *The Magnanimous Month of March*). In his fiction,

the historical novel *Bednyi Avrosimov* (1967–70; *Poor Avro-simov*) is truly thought provoking. It is a human and humane tale about the Decembrist rebels of 1825, showing them not as the superior heroes of the hallowed Russian legend but as ordinary mortals with all their weaknesses. George Reavey aptly remarked about him as a poet: "To read Bulat Okudzhava is to experience a warm, friendly feeling. Here is a poet, who has been through the hell of war and still loves life and song. He sings of love and ordinary people. He also sings of war, but not to glorify it. . . . He is outspoken and sincere. He has a sense of varied rhythm, and his form is plastic and adaptable."

Of the women poets, Bella Akhmadulina was outstanding already in her early twenties. Born in 1937, of unusual Tatar and Italian origin, she was for a time married to Yevtushenko and later to the fiction writer Yuri Nagibin. Even in the permissive year 1957 she was too restless for the Soviet authorities and was then expelled from the student rolls of the Gorky Literary Institute in Moscow. Overcoming the difficulties placed in her path by the officialdom, she achieved publication in *Yunost'* and other magazines, her poems gaining immediate recognition and admiration.

In contrast with Yevtushenko and particularly Voznesensky, she pens her verses in a classical (or near-classical) form. But like most of the new gifted Soviet poets, she bares her intimate emotions in preference to singing of public issues. In 1962 her collection of poems *Struna* (*Chord*) came out to much acclaim. In 1964 her long poem "Moya rodoslovnaya" ("My Genealogy") was loved by her many readers. Of the shorter poems, "Pyatnadtsat' mal'chikov" ("Fifteen Boys") and "Ne udelyai mne mnogo vremeni" ("Don't Devote Much Time to Me") are lightninglike revelations of a woman's sad wisdom about love.

Th less-known Novella Matveyeva (born in 1935, raised in children's homes) began to write in the 1960s. Outstanding is her volume of verse *Dusha veshchei* (1966; *The Soul of Things*). Critics and readers have been attracted by her singular alloy of fantasy and everyday reality, of curiously wild images coupled with proclamations of the need for integrity in the individual.

There is also Rimma Kazakova (born in 1932 in Sevasto-pol) who began to publish her poems in 1955, and soon be-came popular with her romantic lyrics about love, daydreams, restless search for the meaning of life, as well as about sturdy pioneers in Siberia whom she knew from her personal ex-periences in that part of the Soviet Union.

A few women-poets are, in contrast, not young at all, but do try to speak in young voices. The already mentioned Margarita Aligher (real name Makarova, born in 1915 in Odessa) has a middle-rank but pleasingly lyric talent as a poetess. She began to publish in 1933, and her first four col-lections of poems spanned the years 1938–40: *God rozhde-niya* (*The Year of Birth*); *Zima etogo goda* (*The Winter of This Year*); *Zheleznaya doroga* (*The Railroad*); and *Kamni i travy* (*Stones and Grasses*). Official critics at times up-braided her for "a lack of Soviet optimism." A librarian and a literary contributor to a factory newspaper before the Sec-ond World War, she joined the staff of an air force news-paper in wartime. During the war she published five more books of verse, much of it in praise of Red soldiers' bravery. In 1942 she joined the Communist Party. In 1943 she won the Stalin Prize. In 1945 she wrote a play *Skazka o pravde* (*A Fairy Tale about Truth*). In post-Stalinist times her poems pleaded for a liberalization of Soviet life. Her poetic output continued prolific well into the 1960s and '70s.

7

The Forbidden Ones

1 *The Battle against Pasternak*

The time has come to take up such Soviet Russian writers of the 1950s through these 1970s whose work, at least in part, was forbidden in their homeland and in defiance was smuggled into the West, there to be published in Russian as well as in the non-Russian languages. A veritable galaxy of such notably gifted authors were and are still in this category: Pasternak, Sinyavsky, Daniel, Solzhenitsyn, Brodsky, and others.

In describing this phenomenon, we should first of all note that even under the post-Stalin permissiveness, only Stalinism as such was condemned, the aberration of the dictator who had merely distorted the allegedly fine meaning of the original Marxism-Leninism. In retrospect, such protest by most Soviet writers of the middle 1950s seems tame and minor.

Yet, toward the end of this phase, Boris Pasternak's *Doctor Zhivago* was completed and published. It was, however, timidly rejected even by the most liberal Soviet editors of the time and so came out abroad, not in the Soviet Union. Translated into many languages, the novel at once won great acclaim in the outside world. The Party tried to treat this success with silence, but it could no longer do so when in October 1958 Pasternak was awarded that year's Nobel Prize for Literature. Pasternak had been in trouble with government officials before, in the period between the two world wars. As a poet, short-story writer, and autobiographer he had never glorified the revolution.

Pasternak was born in 1890 and died in 1960; his father was a portrait painter who knew Tolstoy, and his mother a concert pianist. Young Boris, educated in Germany, was influenced by two men he had met in his youth, the Czech-German poet Rilke and the Russian composer Alexander Skryabin. Pasternak finally found his own voice as a poet after the First World War—in which he didn't serve because he was partly crippled—and, during the Russian civil war he wrote such verses as those in *Temy i variatsii* (*Themes and Variations*), published in 1923. In that volume, a poem such as "Prorok" ("The Prophet") was hardly calculated to please Party ideologues, since it invoked biblical figures, including the angels out of the Sixth Book of Isaiah and even God, represented as telling the Prophet to go over land and sea to burn the holy words into the hearts of men. Pasternak's vision was one of Pushkin's writing a poem about this, composing it at night and reaching its end as dawn appeared. In the meantime, the phenomena of the earth beat about Pushkin—the Sahara, a port on the White Sea, and the Ganges, as well as man-made objects such as the Sphinx and the Colossus.

> *Stars rushed forth. Headlands washed in seas.*
> *Salt sprays blinded. And tears dried.*
> *Night darkened the bedrooms. Thoughts swarmed.*
> *The Sphinx listened to the Sahara.*
>
> *Candles gleamed. It was as if the blood*
> *Of the Colossus froze. His lips spread wide*
> *With the desert's shadow of blue smile.*
> *Night faded as the tide went out.*
>
> *Breezes from Morocco stroked the sea.*
> *Simoons churned. Archangels snored under snow.*
> *Candles gleamed. The rough draft of "The Prophet"*
> *Dried, and on the Ganges dawn flared up.*

Pasternak's subsequent volume of verse, *God 1905* (1927; *The Year 1905*), though it dealt with the revolt which occurred when Pasternak was fifteen, didn't win the allegiance of Party-line inveterates. Neither did his stories of

Russian life, although the storm didn't explode until 1931, when his autobiography, *Okhrannaya gramota* (*The Safe Conduct*), appeared. This book, with its reminiscences of Rilke and Skryabin and its accounts of university life at Marburg, ending with the horror of Mayakovsky's suicide, didn't glorify the revolution, which received only passing mention, as if it were an unimportant event. The year before *The Safe Conduct* was published, *Pravda* had asserted that literature, films, and other vehicles of artistic expression should be levers which could uplift the masses by giving them examples of the Socialist initiative. Also in 1931, the RAPP stated in its official journal that the only concern of Soviet literature at the time was to tell the story of the Five-Year Plan and the problems of class war connected with it. The Party was then verging toward Socialist realism as an official doctrine and toward the establishment (in 1932) of a single official literary organization, the Union of Soviet Writers. In those years when so many authors received various kinds of punishment from the state, Pasternak was fairly lucky: his autobiography sold out its first edition of 6,200 copies in a short time, and the worst penalty inflicted on him was the suppression of a planned second volume. Nevertheless, volumes of his poems and stories, in "selected" or "collected" editions, continued to come out until the time of the Second World War.

At the first Congress of Soviet Writers in 1934, Pasternak heard himself described by Aleksei Surkov, one of the most minor among minor Soviet versifiers, as a man who could be a great poet if he honored the shining achievement of the revolution. Pasternak's defender at this time, Nikolai Bukharin, was executed four years afterward as a traitor.

In 1935, the principal delegates to the first International Congress of Writers in Defense of Culture astonishingly included Pasternak and Isaac Babel as well as Ilya Ehrenburg. The Paris meetings, ostensibly anti-Fascist, were among the notable Communist-front activities of the time. Pasternak, exhausted by insomnia, launched an oracular speech that had nothing to do with Communism or Fascism. He said that there would always be poetry in the grass (echoing Whitman?), which men would have to bend over to gather, and that if human beings became happier, it would be easier for artists to function. When he was invited to lunch with André Malraux and Jean Cocteau, Pasternak refused. Some reports say that the lunch was scheduled for an hour he didn't regard as convenient, others that he didn't like to watch people eating.

At the 1936 Congress of Soviet Writers, in Minsk, Pasternak was openly defiant: he wouldn't write poetry to order, and he wouldn't travel around reading it to workers; Pushkin, he pointed out, confined his travels to his verse. In that same year—it was the time of the purges—Pasternak refused to sign a statement approving the execution of Marshal Tukhachevsky and others who had fought against the Whites in the civil war, but had fallen into disfavor. Pasternak's wife, who was pregnant, had begged him to sign the document, but he couldn't force himself to do so. Yet when it reached Party headquarters, it contained his name, apparently inserted by a friend who realized the danger to Pasternak if it should be missing. In speaking of this years later, he told a Swedish interviewer that the hierarchy didn't really expect much of one, merely that "you should hate what you like, and love what you abhor."

He further told this interviewer that he regarded the coming of the Second World War as a liberation, an awakening to reality after an evil dream. The sacrifices made in the war would not be meaningless. And the time of conflict brought Pasternak once more into print as a poet. In a volume published in 1943, *Na rannikh poyezdakh* (*On Early Trains*), he named one section of the book "Peredelkino" after the little artists' colony about twenty miles from Moscow, where a *dacha* (country house) had been put at his disposal in 1943 by the Soviet Writers' Union.

Some of the poems from the 1943 volume, along with a dozen new ones, were included two years later in *Zemnoy prostor* (*The Wide Earth*) which, like all Pasternak's later writings, met with official disapproval. In 1946, at the time when Andrei Zhdanov and others were carping at such authors as Zoshchenko, the harshest criticism of Pasternak came from Alexander Fadeyev, for many years his neighbor at Peredelkino. (After the suicide of Fadeyev, a drunkard, in 1956, Pasternak had only kind words for him.) The magazine *Znamya* (*The Banner*) spoke friendlily of Pasternak's war poems, but the Party's Central Committee blamed the Writers' Union for permitting him to be published, since even his war poems were "neutralist" and "individualist."

Pasternak retreated to his wooden house at Peredelkino amid the orchards and the groves of firs. He worked on his novel and on his translation of Goethe's *Faust*. He brought out no more volumes of poetry during his lifetime, and even those he had published were out of print, yet his work was known: people copied it by hand, and many committed it to memory. Ilya Ehrenburg told some visitors from abroad that even though Pasternak's poems were not then on sale in the Soviet Union, people would come from all over Russia, perhaps as many as twenty thousand, walking if they had to—if Pasternak would give a public reading of his verse. For he was the great poet of their land. Often difficult to read, with his extensive use of metonymy and symbol, of subtle metaphor, he was nevertheless known as a poet of magnitude.

His poetic talent served him well in *Dr. Zhivago*, not merely because the book is written with the color and rhythm which some poets can expertly carry over into prose without making the latter too obviously "poetic." But he did add to the novel an epilogue containing normal poetry, supposedly written by Zhivago, who was both doctor and poet.

This novel took about twenty years to write, before its completion in 1955. When, three years later, Pasternak was awarded the Nobel Prize for Literature, he was the second Russian to receive this honor; as mentioned earlier, the first was the émigré Ivan Bunin. Now, in late 1958, Khrushchev and his Party ordered a campaign of attack and abuse upon both the Nobel Committee and Pasternak. The Party's official handmaiden, the Union of Soviet Writers, lunged forth obediently. Presently, humiliated and frightened, Pasternak was forced to recant, to refuse the Prize, and to plead his loyalty to the régime smiting him. The few remaining years of his life and work at Peredelkino were fairly miserable.

The Party of course had a reason for its persecution of Pasternak: in his epic novel he went to the root of Stalinism —to the entire premise and unfulfilled promise of Marx and Lenin, when, through the words of Yuri Andreyevich Zhivago, the novelist said: "Marxism is too uncontrolled to be a science. Sciences are more balanced. . . . I don't know a movement more centered and further removed from the facts than Marxism."

It was true that Zhivago—Pasternak—offered no other definite sociopolitical system of thought and action to replace the failed Marxism-Leninism. But he did offer a philosophy—that of nature and its depth and beauty, of love and individualism. The novel's implied hope was that, out of these, mankind would someday somehow mould a better sociopolitics than Communism could ever offer.

After Khrushchev was deposed by Brezhnev in 1964 he had time for second thoughts. Shortly before his death in 1971 he dictated a tape (first made public in the West—but not in the Soviet Union—in May 1974), confessing that he had never read *Doctor Zhivago* but had followed his aides' strong advice to ban the novel and abuse Pasternak, and voicing his regret of his error. He practically apologized to Pasternak's memory ("Better late than never"), adding: "While personally I'm against the new schools of painting, sculpture, and music, that doesn't mean I see any need for resorting to administrative and police measures."

2   *The Case of Sinyavsky and Daniel*

It was in 1956 that two Soviet writers, Andrei Sinyavsky and Yuli Daniel, both thirty-one years old then, and both not members of the Communist Party, began to show to their trusted friends certain of their manuscripts. These could not be published in the Soviet Union because they were highly and bitingly critical of the Party and the Soviet system. The pair knew that all around them were spies and informers, yet, fearlessly, they took risks.

They risked even more when, through a certain contact,

they began to send their stories and essays across the borders to the West, where their work soon was freely printed, in the original Russian and many translations, Sinyavsky's texts under the pseudonym of "Abram Tertz," Daniel's as "Nikolai Arzhak."

Sinyavsky's writings thus published abroad included a novelette *Sud idyot* (1956; *Here Comes the Court*; in English, 1960, *The Trial Begins*) exposing the entire repressive essence of the so-called Soviet justice; a novelette *Lyubimov* (1962–63; *The City of Lyubimov*), dissecting the inhumanity of the Soviet way of life and death; and an essay, *What Is Socialist Realism?*, attacking the Party's role in literature and other arts.

Daniel's Western editions comprised a novelette *Govorit Moskva* (1961; *Moscow Is Speaking*), a horrifying fantasy of the Day of Open Murder, ostensibly declared by the Soviet government on a certain date in 1961; also *Chelovek iz MINAP'a* (*A Man from Minap*) and *Iskupleniye* (*Redemption*), two indictments of the Soviet people no less than of the Soviet system—the people who allowed such a system to enslave them.

These Western editions were smuggled into the Soviet Union and circulated secretly but widely, much to the consternation of the Party's oligarchs and their police. The authorities raged at their inability to track down the real identities of "Tertz" and "Arzhak" and the channels through which their manuscripts made their way westward, to return home as books to delight the Soviet reader.

The wonder was that Sinyavsky and Daniel kept all this up for nine long years. But finally, in 1965, the KGB (as the Soviet secret police are called) did uncover a few important clues (in part, it was rumored, with the aid of computers calculating and comparing the frequency of words in the pair's styles). In November 1965, the two were arrested. In February 1966, they were tried in Moscow on charges of engaging in anti-Soviet agitation.

During the trial it was made known that the pair's main "window to the West" was Mme Hélène Peltier-Zamoyska, the daughter of a French naval attaché. While in Moscow,

she studied Russian literature, particularly the prerevolutionary work of Leonid Andreyev. In the early 1960s it was she
who secretly transported to Western publishers the writings
of Sinyavsky and Daniel. When the prosecutor spoke of the
"awfulness" of sending manuscripts out of the USSR "with
the aid of the naval attaché's daughter," Daniel calmly re-
joined: "I relayed them through Zamoyska, but as to whose
daughter she was, this didn't interest me." Both were found
guilty and sentenced to concentration-camp imprisonment:
Sinyavsky to seven years, Daniel to five years.

To the shame of the Soviet world of letters be it said that
eventually, in a public speech, Mikhail Sholokhov expressed
his regret that Sinyavsky and Daniel had not been sentenced
to death by shooting. And to the despair of all men of good
will and decency be it noted that in 1965 Sholokhov was
awarded the Nobel Prize in Literature.

After six years in the slave camp, Sinyavsky was released.
In the summer of 1973 he was allowed to leave for France,
to teach at the Sorbonne in Paris. On arrival in the West
he refused all interviews, saying that he was no longer concerned with politics. Yet, in the same year of 1973, a London
publishing house issued his book *Golos iz khora* (A *Voice
from the Choir*), consisting mainly of his letters to his wife
from the concentration camp. Daniel, released earlier, remained in the Soviet Union in obscurity.

3   Some Years in the Life of Alexander Solzhenitsyn

The writings of Alexander Solzhenitsyn, the Nobel
laureate since 1970, have been even more profound and
world famous. Indeed, Solzhenitsyn is so famous that the
oligarchs didn't dare to arrest him. He was harassed, cursed,
and humiliated. His manuscripts were seized from him by
the KGB. The Union of Soviet Writers, on orders from the
Kremlin, canceled his membership. He was made an outcast
in his own country—he, his nation's greatest living writer—
and finally expelled in 1974, on charges of treason. This oc-

curred after Western publication of *The Gulag Archipelago,*
1918–1956, his documentary history of Soviet prison camps,
a book we will discuss later.

Born in 1918, by his early training and profession a teacher
of physics, Solzhenitsyn served in the Second World War as
an artillery officer, but was toward its end arrested and sentenced to slave labor for writing a few disrespectful words
about Stalin in a private letter, which was intercepted by the
secret police. In literature he began in 1962 as a total unknown. Emerging from years in northern concentration
camps and Central Asian exile, ill with cancer, he described
the slavery he had suffered and seen in a novelette *Odin den'*
Ivana Denisovicha (One Day in the Life of Ivan Deniso-
vich). The manuscript came to the notice of Alexander
Tvardovsky, himself a questioning writer and poet, then the
editor of the foremost Soviet monthly *Novy mir,* a magazine
of liberal tendencies. He later said that, starting to read Solzhenitsyn's story late one evening, he couldn't put it down
until he finished it, and was so excited that he didn't sleep at
all that night. It took subtle pressures upon Khrushchev,
with the help of his daughter and son-in-law, to gain permission for *One Day's* publication.

The novella appeared in *Novy mir* for November 1962 and
became a countrywide sensation. The issue was sold out at
once. Lines of people stood at the libraries, simply to be put
on the waiting list for that magazine. Three or four more
stories by Solzhenitsyn were soon published. The nation and
the world knew that a writer of great power and moral
strength had emerged. The Party was alarmed. No more
work by Solzhenitsyn was to be published.

Solzhenitsyn's novel *Rakovyi korpus (The Cancer Ward)*
was accepted by Tvardovsky nevertheless. It was to be
printed in *Novy mir* for January 1968; the type was set. But
Khrushchev's heirs, Leonid Brezhnev and Aleksei Kosygin,
pronounced their veto. One and a half years later Tvardovsky
lost his editorship of *Novy mir.* Heartbroken and ill, he died
in December 1971.

The few of Solzhenitsyn's works that were legally published in the USSR during the brief Khrushchevian permis-

siveness (such as *One Day in the Life of Ivan Denisovich*, also those few short stories) are now black-marketed at about ten times their original list prices.

Neither *The Cancer Ward* nor Solzhenitsyn's other two powerful novels—*V kruge pervom* (1968; *The First Circle*) and *Avgust chetyrnadtsatogo* (1971; *August 1914*)—have to this day been published in the Soviet Union. Printed abroad, translated into many languages, they make their clandestine way back to the eager Soviet reader, to supplement the many typewritten *samizdat* (underground press) copies circulating from one end of the nation to the other.

In subject matter, *The First Circle* closely follows *One Day in the Life of Ivan Denisovich*. Both are accounts of life and struggle in Stalinist slave camps. But if *One Day* is a general protest against this inhumanity to humans, *The First Circle* is a more specific indictment of enslavement of scientists and engineers, the Communist debasement of education in its most lofty and refined forms—of physics, mathematics, and electronics. Yet both books are of a piece in their revelation of the Stalinist inferno, in their deepest psychological insights and their highest moral and artistic terms.

The Cancer Ward is a vehicle of protest on a somewhat different level. Its protagonist is a cancer patient come to the ward from the primitive Kazakhstan steppes where he is in exile following his slave-camp years. This novel, similarly autobiographic, is movingly realistic yet also symbolic as its individual portraits of patients and doctors merge into a collective picture of the Soviet society of the 1960s—a microcosm of the society that is one gigantic sick ward, the great nation that is all cancerous.

August 1914, written in a very different style from Solzhenitsyn's other novels and stories, is a giant effort by the author to bring back the memory of the Russian part in the early phases of the First World War—and, apparently, to show a contrast between the heroic sacrifices of his people and the ineptitude and criminality of their imperial leaders, whom Solzhenitsyn holds in as much contempt as he does Soviet Russia's oligarchs. This book is the first of a series; the next phase of Russia's history in which he will place his heroes and villains of 1914 is planned by him for the year 1916. Despite all the handicaps placed by the Communist government in the path of his research and writing, Solzhenitsyn kept on writing the story of 1916.

The Nobel award of late 1970 caused a new outburst of the Party's venom against Solzhenitsyn. The anti-Pasternak witch-hunt chorus of 1958–59 was played over again. But in 1970–71, unlike Pasternak, Solzhenitsyn did not break. Proudly he accepted the Prize; for a while he contemplated journeying to Stockholm to receive it in person. But he soon decided against the trip, and among his reasons he cited his conviction that the Party would not let him return to his beloved homeland were he to leave it even temporarily. Yet, as he made his sad decision known, he continued to stand above the Party's henchmen, his body erect, his head and spirit high, not for a moment lessening his firm resolve to be his people's conscience unafraid.

In 1972 the text of Solzhenitsyn's lecture, prepared for delivery at the acceptance of the Prize in Stockholm, was smuggled out of the Soviet Union, widely published in the West, and later found its way back for underground distribution in his homeland. A beautifully written speech, it is a plea for the indivisibility of freedom throughout the world, and an assurance that "writers and artists can conquer falsehood." The truth will eventually prevail; "falsehood can hold out against much in this world, but not against art."

In August 1973 Solzhenitsyn publicly, in ringing tones, protested against the prohibition by the Soviet secret police for him to live in Moscow where his wife and two infant sons were legal residents: "Serfdom in our country was abolished 112 years ago and, it is said, the October Revolution wiped out its last remnants. I am neither a serf nor a slave and should be free to live wherever I find it necessary, and no one, not even the highest authorities, should have the proprietory right to separate me from my family."

He reminded the world that millions of other Soviet citizens, particularly the nation's peasants, were forbidden to choose their place of residence, to move freely in their own homeland, a deplorable situation that "probably does not

exist even in the colonial countries of the world of today."
He demanded freedom of movement for everybody, not just
for himself.

Also in August 1973 Solzhenitsyn revealed that he had
been receiving repeated threats against his life, which letters
and telephone calls—although anonymous—quite evidently
originated with the Soviet secret police. He announced that
even if he were murdered his voice would not be stilled: for
he had by then managed to relay to his Western friends certain of his important manuscripts, ready to be published
posthumously.

But he had numerous staunch friends also at home in the
Soviet land. In helping Solzhenitsyn to survive in the hostile surroundings erected around him by the Soviet secret
police, true courage was manifested by, among others, the
famous Soviet cellist Mstislav Rostropovich when in 1970–71
he proudly acknowledged his friendship to Solzhenitsyn, to
whom he gave refuge in his house outside Moscow and in
whose defense against the government's attacks on the writer
he came out in several ringing public statements. For this
advocacy the cellist was punished: the government canceled
the foreign concert tour for which Rostropovich was scheduled beginning in late 1970.

In September 1973 Solzhenitsyn, in a statement to Western correspondents in Moscow, revealed that a Leningrad
woman had been forced by the KGB after five days of stringent questioning to divulge the whereabouts of a major underground manuscript of his, which she had typed, dealing
with the Party's terrorism of Stalinist times. Some two hundred survivors of that terror, who had supplied Solzhenitsyn
with these historic details in the early 1960s, were now en-
dangered. The unfortunate woman could not stand the
thought of the betrayal for which she was responsible in her
weakness. Solzhenitsyn said, "On her return home, she
hanged herself."

Yet Solzhenitsyn had taken the precaution of secretly
sending to Western Europe a copy of this manuscript. Now,
realizing that the KGB possessed a copy of its own, which
it might put to its peculiar uses, Solzhenitsyn signaled to his

Western friends to go ahead with the publication of the book. This was how the sensational volume, *The Gulag Archipelago, 1918–1956*, was published first by the Russian émigré house in Paris, the IMKA Press, in December 1973, and in its numerous translations all over the free world, including English, in the spring of 1974. (The name IMKA is the Russian transliteration of the YMCA publishing organization which founded this émigré unit before the Second World War.)

The book is based largely on the hundreds of letters and verbal accounts which former political prisoners of the Lenin and Stalin times sent to Solzhenitsyn after his Ivan Denisovich had first spoken to his fellow Russians and to the outside world. To these bitter documents Solzhenitsyn added his own reminiscences, thus making the narrative in part autobiographical. It is not fiction, it is history; but its impassioned pages move the book as a powerful novel by a great master surely would. One striking feature of the book is Solzhenitsyn's condemnation not just of Stalin, but also of Lenin, for these crimes against humanity. Solzhenitsyn's careful yet wrathful analysis shows that Lenin was the one who began the system of slavery and executions.

The resulting uproar shook the world. The Soviet government launched an unprecedented campaign of villification against Solzhenitsyn, while the most progressive men and women of the world at large raised their voices to support the author and to warn the Communists not to harm him. On February 12, 1974 the police arrested Solzhenitsyn and accused him of treason, an offense punishable by death in the Soviet Union. But on the following day they exiled him, and he went to West Germany to stay with his friend and fellow Nobel laureate, Heinrich Böll. Soon afterward, Solzhenitsyn moved to Switzerland, where he was joined by his family.

He continued working on his series of novels about the First World War which had begun with *August 1914*. One important point to be noted, among others, about Solzhenitsyn is his protest against the official Soviet prohibition of the writing of the word *God* with a capital G. In his afterword to

August 1914 Solzhenitsyn declares that this book can be published abroad, but not in the Soviet Union, not only because of "the senseless Soviet censorship," but also because "it would have been necessary to write the word 'God' with the first letter in a lower case, and to this humiliation I cannot bend."

Despite the ban decreed against his works by the Communist leaders, Solzhenitsyn today is a prime factor not alone in the conscience of the Soviet people but also in the language of his fellow countrymen. As his books, published abroad in Russian, are smuggled into the USSR and ceaselessly circulated among its eager readers, in content his novels and stories call for freedom, and in language they are a vivid, vital protest against the dreary official Russian style of both writing and speaking in his land.

Among his other methods Solzhenitsyn experiments by bringing into his writings the rough, tough speech of concentration camps which he has known at first hand as a prisoner in Stalinist days; the frank, desperate cries of cancer wards where he has been a patient; the unadorned colloquialisms and slang, the inner poetry and outward cynicism of the peasants, workers, intellectuals, and all the other mix and mélange of the populace with whom he has lived and slaved and suffered; of the Russians, those majority speakers of the great Russian language, and the many non-Russians, the so-called "national minorities"—the Jews, the Ukrainians, the Estonians, the Uzbeks and all the scores of other ethnic groups who contribute their own flavor to the speech and writing of the Russians. All in all, it is a most candid and colorful language that emerges from Solzhenitsyn's pages, but though frank and rough, it is always skillfully experimental, never stupidly excremental.

Solzhenitsyn also experiments by digging into the musty volumes of old nineteenth-century dictionaries of folk Russian, rural Russian, regional Russian, and by putting all that wondrous vocabulary and all that half-forgotten but still viable syntax into the mouths of his heroes and anti-heroes, taking care nonetheless that such revived archaic words and phrase-turns fit naturally, that no error is committed by making a clerk or an engineer use a peasant locution or vice versa, that no change of syntax is too artificial-seeming.

Following Solzhenitsyn's lead, many other Russian writers, particularly in the underground *samizdat,* try to write colorfully, pungently, juicily. And, inevitably, an intense argument is already roaring about and around this use by Solzhenitsyn and his followers of this kind of unusual, revived, and changed language.

All to the good, we can rightly say. In the eighteenth century Mikhail Lomonosov, Russia's first eminent physicist, chemist, and linguist, wrote that the Russian language even then had "the splendor of Spanish, the vivacity of French, the strength of German, the tenderness of Italian, and the richness and brevity of Greek and Latin." In the nineteenth century Ivan Turgenev, the novelist, called his native language "a great, mighty, truthful, and free tongue." Today, as we near the end of the third quarter of the twentieth century, Alexander Solzhenitsyn is proving how right both Lomonosov and Turgenev were, how appropriate their praise can be for the present-day Russian language, in spite of what totalitarian politics have done or tried to do to it since 1917.

4   The Union of Nonconformity

Among the other, less illustrious yet significant Russian writers banned in their homeland, the poet Iosif Brodsky (born in 1940) is well known. He has tried to be nonpolitical; he proclaimed metaphysics as his essence. He claimed receiving an enthusiastic approval from Anna Akhmatova in her last years, although it is clear that she was not an influence upon his style and themes. He sought kinship in Alexander Blok's early poetry, and also in the English verse of John Donne and the Polish poems of Adam Mickiewiz, both of whom he read in the original and translated. George L. Kline writes of Brodsky: "His muse is personal, meditative, religious, 'suffering.' He is obsessed with the mysteries of love, death, communion, solitude, sin, and salvation. Almost alone among Soviet poets of his generation, he is uncontaminated by Mayakovskyan bombast, braggadocio, and hyperbole." In March 1964 Brodsky was publicly tried for "parasitism" and sentenced to five years of exile and manual labor in the north. In 1972 he was allowed to emigrate to the United States where he became a poet in residence and a lecturer at the University of Michigan. None of his poems is permitted publication in the Soviet Union. Two of his volumes were published in New York: *Stikhotvoreniya i poemy* (1965; *Verses and Poems*) and *Ostanovka v pustyne* (1970; *A Halt in the Desert*). English translations of Brodsky's poems by George L. Kline and others are scattered in various American periodicals and anthologies.

Lidiya Chukovskaya, daughter of the old and much-respected writer Kornei Chukovsky, is herself a powerful creator of fiction. In 1939–40 she had written a novelette *Opustelyi dom* (*The Deserted House*), but she knew it could not be published then. Moreover, had the manuscript been found in her desk, she would have been arrested for it by the secret police and shipped off to a slave camp. For it was the story of a woman losing her son to the Stalinist prisons. Yet, even after Stalin's death, it was too strong a narrative to be published in the Soviet Union. So it was taken abroad, and published in Russian in Paris in 1965 (it achieved its English publication in London in 1967).

Neither could Chukovskaya's next outstanding work, her novelette *Spusk pod vodu* (*Descent under the Water*), be printed in the Soviet Union legally. It appeared in typewritten copies in *samizdat*, Russia's underground press, in 1972 (the printed book was soon published in the West). The scene of this story is a house of rest near Moscow; the time is the late 1940s; the book's aim is again the author's protest against the inhumanity of the Soviet system.

In January 1974, for her writings as well as her fearless public stand in defense and praise of Andrei Sakharov and other Soviet dissidents, Chukovskaya was expelled from the Union of Soviet Writers—on orders from the Kremlin rulers.

Another rebellious writer of modern Soviet days, Vladimir Maksimov (Samsonov), is the son of a peasant who had become a Moscow factory worker. He was born in 1932 but hardly knew his father, for the elder Maksimov was arrested and sent off to a concentration camp, from which he was released only in 1939, to be first a miner, then a Red Army soldier, soon to die at the front. Young Vladimir's childhood was one of extreme poverty, and at fifteen he left home. The itinerant youth was repeatedly arrested and kept in children's detention centers, also in jails for juveniles. At eighteen he became a surveyor in North Siberia, then a construction worker all over Russia, and later a jack-of-all-trades on a *kolkhoz* in the Northern Caucasus.

All the time he observed, he read, he wrote. In his early twenties he became a peripatetic journalist, but at last found his true literary path with a collection of verse *Pokoleniye na chasakh* (1956; *The Generation on Sentry Duty*). Paustovsky noticed and encouraged his talent by including Maksimov's first novelette "My obzhivayem zemlyu" ("We Make the Land Our Home") in his almanac *Tarusskiye stranitsy* (1961; *Tarusa Pages*). Despite the writer's tragic plots suffused with a spirit of protest against the Soviet system, Maksimov's work was allowed to be published, for those were still the comparatively mild Khrushchevian times.

In 1962 his novel *Zhiv chelovek* (*Man Alive*) drew much attention, was subsequently translated into a number of foreign languages, and in 1965 made into a play produced by the Pushkin Drama Theater in Moscow. A bitterly truthful portrayal of life and death under Stalin in the 1930s, it attracted capacity audiences for several years, and finally the Brezhnev-Kosygin régime ordered it to be removed from the stage. A campaign of persecution was launched against Maksimov. His further work was banned. He was repeatedly summoned for examinations by the KGB doctors "to check his sanity." In the summer of 1973 he was expelled from the Union of Soviet Writers.

Maksimov's eloquent protests were smuggled out and made public in the West. Of his latest writings, the novel *Sem' dnei tvoreniya* (*Seven Days of Creation*), a family chronicle embracing more than a half-century of disillusioned and otherwise negative life under the Soviets, appeared in Russian in 1971 in West Germany and was later translated into several languages. His next novel, *Karantin* (*Quarantine*), similarly critical of the Communist system, and also forbidden in the Soviet Union, was published in Russian in 1973 by the same West German house of the sympathetic émigrés. It was in the same summer of 1973 that Maksimov caused a sensation by writing a public letter to the West German novelist Heinrich Böll, the 1972 Nobel Prize laureate, in which the Soviet writer accused Chancellor Willy Brandt of West Germany of making it possible for Brezhnev to worsen the denial of civil liberties in the Soviet Union through the Chancellor's policy of détente with the Soviet rulers. (Böll was selected by Maksimov as the addressee apparently because the German writer had earlier denounced the Soviet rulers for their persecution of that country's dissident writers and other nonconformists and had in turn been castigated by the official Soviet propagandists.) In early 1974 Maksimov was given a passport and an exit visa, and he left for the West. The expectation was that should he wish to return home to Russia the Soviet government would refuse to let him in, and would even lift his passport and deprive him of his citizenship, thus making him an émigré, a practice recently introduced by the Kremlin in its effort to get rid of dissidents.

A thoughtful critic will note that Soviet dissidence is incomplete if it protests certain current revivals of Stalinism, if it decries what Brezhnev and Kosygin do to the freedoms of Soviet citizens, if it denounces Stalin and his work and heritage—but absolves Lenin. If this dissidence does not really, deeply analyze Lenin's personality and role in creating the injustices and the inequalities of the long decades of the Soviet régime, then this dissidence still does not perform fully and profoundly enough.

In the 1960s and '70s at least two works of fiction appeared in the Soviet underground, in its typewritten *samizdat*, which boldly take up this task of dissecting and denouncing Lenin and Leninism. One is an anonymous typescript circulated among Soviet readers, entitled "Smuta noveishego vremeni ili udivitel'nyie pokhozhdeniya Vani Chmotanova" ("The Disturbances of Recent Days or the Amazing Adventures of Vanya Chmotanov"). The original text began to make its way from reader to reader sometime in 1970. Smuggled out to the West, it was printed in the Paris Russian-language weekly *Russkaya mysl'* (*Russian Thought*) in November 1970. (Its English translation was printed in *Survey, a Journal of East & West Studies*, London, Summer 1971, as "*Samizdat*: Troubles of Recent Times or the Amazing Adventures of Vanya Chmotanov.")

A story of a professional thief who happens to resemble Lenin in his youth, it leads to a hilarious satire on the deified leader and a bitter attack on the sociopolitical house he founded. With its frank and acid sallies against Lenin, this anonymous tale is far more than a protest against the excessiveness of the Lenin cult—it is an earthy, mighty cry against the Big Brother himself.

The other anti-Lenin work is the far more artistically presented *Vsyo techyot* (in English, 1972, *Forever Flowing*) by Vasily Grossman (1905–64). An engineer-chemist by training and profession, whose early writings were noticed and liked by Maxim Gorky, in the 1930s Grossman had tried to be a loyal Soviet writer. At that time he was highly praised by those in power. But in the 1940s he was attacked by the Party's henchmen as a Jew, "a cosmopolite," and a man not exactly faithful to the Soviet cause. In 1946 his play *Yesli verit' pifagoreitsam* (*If We Are to Believe the Pythagoreans*) was banned. In 1953 *Pravda* unleashed a campaign against him for the very first chapters of a novel *Za pravoye delo* (*For the Right Cause*) published in *Novy mir* in July–October 1952. Its printing was interrupted and remained unfinished. Other of Grossman's writings were seized by the secret police and are unpublished to this day. His *Forever Flowing* was apparently written just before he died in 1964, in a bitter, desperate mood, as if feeling that he had nothing more to lose.

This is a novel about a man called Ivan Grigoryevich, who returns to Moscow, Leningrad, and other Soviet cities as a free man after thirty cruel and unjust years in Arctic slave camps. A calm, yet overwhelming book, it gives the reader a series of true-to-life stories of Stalinist inhumanity and post-Stalinist hypocrisy. But the most remarkable feature of the narrative is Grossman's approach to Lenin: to date it is the most searing anti-Leninism in the Soviet Union's underground literature. And yet, in this novel, Grossman does not present Lenin as a completely negative man. He points out that in the existing lore and writings on Lenin, two Lenins emerge, and that he, Grossman, adds another. He writes:

> The first is the familiar deified image. The second is the version created by his enemies: the monolithic simpleton, combining the cruel characteristics of the leader of a new world order with equally primitive crude traits in his everyday life. These were the only traits his enemies could see in him.

But Grossman in his novel gives us his "third Lenin, who seems [to him] the closest to actual reality—and this Lenin is not by any means easy to comprehend." So he balances "Lenin's endearing, humane and human qualities" with his appalling traits of "absolute intolerance . . . rancor, pitilessness," rejection of freedom for anyone except himself. The result is an evil genius, a monster, bad news for the deceived and betrayed mankind.

For its political message no less than its artistic fiber *Forever Flowing* will (or at least should be) singled out as one of the truly epochal works not alone in the Soviet letters, but in world literature as well. In its anti-Lenin message it was forcefully joined in 1973–74 by Solzhenitsyn's *The Gulag Archipelago*.

5   *Later Theater and Film*

Both the theater and the motion picture have had their ups and downs in the Soviet Union since Stalin's death. In the de-Stalinization period of the latter 1950s and early '60s a few plays were written and staged against "the personality cult" and other inequities of Stalin's time. Gradually, especially after Khrushchev's downfall in October 1964, this libertarian wave receded and disappeared. A particularly daring play or two was denounced by the Party in Khrushchev's reign. Typically, in July 1961, Marshal Filip I. Golikov, head of the Chief Political Office of the armed forces, denounced Alexander Shtein for his play about the Soviet navy, *Okean* (*The Ocean*), then running simultaneously in several theaters in Moscow and elsewhere. The play, the marshal complained, applauded such "vices" of the Soviet military personnel as refusal to inform on one another.

No such bold front can be detected on the Soviet stage in these Brezhnev-Kosygin times. And in the current Russian theater, for obvious reasons, no plays of the nonconformist category can be produced even in secrecy. The smallest cast and the tiniest audience would inevitably draw the attention of neighbors and informers. Banned plays do appear, however, as typewritten *samizdat*. Such has been the lot of *Olen' i shalashovka* (*The Naïve One and the Prostitute*, translated into English as *The Love-Girl and the Innocent*), Solzhenitsyn's play about tragic love in a slave camp; also of his play with a similar bitter subject, *Pir pobeditelei* (*Feast of the Conquerors*); as well as his play with a non-Russian locale, *Svecha na vetru* (*Candle in the Wind*). None of these three plays has been produced in the Soviet Union. All three have been read in countless typewritten copies in sub-rosa gatherings of Solzhenitsyn's admirers in that country—and staged in the West. Solzhenitsyn himself, while dearly wishing to see *The Love-Girl and the Innocent* and *Candle in the Wind* some day allowed on the Soviet stage, has an entirely different feeling about *Feast of the Conquerors*, which he wrote while he was Stalin's prisoner: he regrets this play emphatically, terming it a momentary mistake committed in excessive bitterness, an eclipse of his creative sun, so to say.

Not that the latest Soviet theater is entirely bereft of life. Such comparatively enlightened current producer-directors as Yuri Lyubimov and Georgy Tovstonogov try to present such questing playwrights as Aleksei Arbuzov and Eduard Radzinsky. Arbuzov, particularly, although no longer young, continues to write mildly challenging plays. Born in Moscow in 1908, a graduate of a Leningrad drama school, he was first published in 1930, had his first play produced in 1935 (*Dal'-nyaya doroga*, or *The Distant Road*), and showed his later work in the dramas *Irkutskaya istoriya* (1959; *The Irkutsk Story*); *Moy bednyi Marat* (1965; *My Poor Marat*, known in the Western theater as *The Promise*); and *Nochnaya ispoved'* (1967; *Confession in the Night*). One of Arbuzov's main themes is formation of the spiritual personality of Soviet young people. The Brezhnev-Kosygin officialdom does not quite like some of the questioning in this playwright's texts; still, his plays are permitted.

But a stage review of timid topicality, of which Andrei Voznesensky was co-author, was banned after a few performances. A rather unexpected bright spot in the dreary Soviet theater of the 1970s is the play *Voskhozhdeniye na Fudzhiyamu* (*The Ascent of Fujiyama*), on which the well-known Kirghiz novelist Chinghiz Aimatov collaborated. Frankly, yet sensitively, it raises the problem of individual and collective responsibility of Soviet citizens for the crimes of Stalinism. The wonder is that this drama, playing to packed houses, has been permitted by the Brezhnev régime.

As for the cinema, in the post-Stalin times a few superior films were made by Grigory Chukhrai, Mikhail Kalatozov, and others. *Letyat zhuravli* (1957; *The Cranes Are Flying*) and *Ballada o soldate* (1959; *Ballad of a Soldier*) stand out for this period. The early 1960s ushered in an angry Party campaign against too much liberalism in Soviet films. Hence orders from above came to the subservient critics to denounce *Mir vkhodyashchemu* (1961; *Peace to the One Who Enters*), a film about the closing days of the Second World War and the Soviet troops in Germany, as "excessively" pacifist and "treating our army life incorrectly."

From December 1962 through March 1963 Khrushchev himself led a shrill onslaught on his film makers who had just then been completing *Zastava Ilyicha* (*The Lenin Outpost*) wherein young Soviet citizens, both civilian and military, were represented as doubting the moral worth of the Soviet military effort. *The Lenin Outpost* was banned, and the version which has since then, in post-Khrushchev times, emerged to the Soviet screen surely lacks its pristine pacifist touch. In the spring of 1963 the Party waged a determined campaign also against the Soviet film *U tvoyego poroga* (*At Your Doorstep*), which dealt with the early phase of Hitler's invasion of Russia. A decorated veteran acted as the Party's mouthpiece in *Komsomolśkaya pravda* of March 31 when he attacked the film's makers for "its pessimism and despair emanating from the soldiers' each movement and word, as if these were not Soviet men but the heroes of 'the lost generation' entering the film from Remarque's bitter pages." A Red soldier in the film was heard saying that war "is an unnatural phenomenon, not inherent in man." The Party spokesman was angry: "But there are different kinds of war. Our army conducts a war that is holy and just." This film, too, was first banned, then released after much cutting.

From 1969 on, the remarkable Soviet color film *Andrei Rublyov* has been under partial prohibition in the Soviet Union—although in 1969–70 it could be seen in five theaters in Paris, from which the Soviet government frantically but unsuccessfully tried to withdraw it. Rublyov, who lived from about 1360 to 1430, was a genius, a deeply religious Russian icon painter whose work has not been surpassed over the centuries. In deciding to ban this film, the Party obviously regretted the brief lapse into permissiveness that had made it possible for a team of Soviet moviemakers to produce this masterpiece in praise of great religious art as well as in condemnation of ancient Russians' unlovely ways—too suggestive an allusion to modern Russians' moral defects. Still, in these middle 1970s, a limited public exhibition of this film in the Soviet Union is finally being allowed.

8

Anatomy of Dissent

1 Collective Disagreement

In the preceding chapters we have seen that not all the Soviet denizens—particularly men and women of the arts—accept the régime unquestionably at all times. But the dissent we have indicated is seldom aggressive or even active. Rather, it is of the passive kind, beat-the-Soviet-law sort, often insidious and effective, yet not effective enough really to endanger the Soviet state and society as these have existed since 1917.

To be sure, in the past there were uprisings of the general population, but these came very early in the Soviet era—most notably the Tambov and Kronstadt rebellions of 1920–21. And they were all ruthlessly quelled, never to be tried again. General Andrei Vlasov's movement of former Soviet soldiers against the Communist régime during the Second World War is not to be counted as a spontaneous insurgence within the USSR. This occurred outside the territory then dominated by the Soviet government and its troops; and it would have been impossible without the Nazi plan and effort to help organize those former prisoners. After the war, on Soviet soil itself, there were short and bloody strikes and riots such as those of the slaves at Vorkuta in 1953 and of the workers at Novocherkassk in 1962, but these were isolated and brief flare-ups with never a chance of engulfing even a single province.

And yet, dissent has continued in the Soviet Union, dissent of two kinds, both unique. One involves individual action. The other is a mass effort. Both are attempted by intellectuals more generally and frequently than by any other class.

The first category is that of defection. (Let us note the unsatisfactory quality of the word *defection* as applied in the West to those who, disagreeing with the Communist Party and the Soviet régime, escape from the USSR. You do not defect from something you do not believe in. The word *escape* is much more accurate. Yet, even in the present book *defection* is occasionally used because of the custom.) That defection exists is, of course, nothing new. Its beginnings date back to the earliest 1920s when individual Soviet diplomats or professors or men and women of the arts would decline to return home from their missions abroad. From then on, well into the 1960s, *nevozvrashchentsy* or "non-returners," and *perebezhchiki* or "crossers-over" excited the curiosity and, often, sympathy of the West. What is so different about the latest additions to these ranks is the high station of some of them. Apparently the fame and comforts and even luxuries they enjoyed at home didn't make up for the sense of freedom they keenly missed. There was Rudolf Nureyev, the exquisite ballet dancer, who refused to return to the Soviet Union from Paris in 1961. There was the extraordinary case of Svetlana Alliluyeva, Stalin's own daughter, who dramatically defected in India in 1967. Two gifted writers, Arkady and Natalia Belinkov (man and wife), refused to come back from the West in 1968. On a Kremlin-blessed trip to London the well-known writer Anatoly Kuznetsov crossed over in 1969. He was followed, also in London, by that talented ballerina Natalia Makarova in 1970. And in June 1971 the space-electronics expert Anatoly Fedoseyev left the Soviet delegation at the air show in Paris to become a free man.

The second rubric of nonpassive dissent is even more spectacular. For this needs a more complex organization than individual protest and flight; it is a collective dissent, by groups of bold people engaged in underground action. This is the already mentioned *samizdat*, or publication by Soviet citizens of literature forbidden by the Party and the government. We have touched upon it briefly at various points of the preceding chapters. Here is the time and the place to dwell upon it in detail as one of the most significant developments in the Soviet state and society in recent times.

2   *Journalism of the Clandestine*

Censorship existed even before literature, according to the Russians. And, we may add, censorship being older, literature has to be craftier. Hence, the new and remarkably viable underground press in the Soviet Union called *samizdat*. The word is a play on *Gosizdat*, which is a telescoping of *Gosudarstvennoye izdatel'stvo*, the name of the monopoly-wielding State Publishing House. The *sam* part of the new word means "self." The whole—*samizdat*—translates as: "We publish ourselves"—that is, not the state, but we, the people.

Unlike the underground of tsarist times, today's *samizdat* has no printing presses (with rare exceptions): the KGB, the secret police, is too efficient. It is the typewriter, each page produced with four to eight carbon copies, that does the job. By the thousands and tens of thousands of frail, smudged onionskin sheets, *samizdat* spreads across the land a mass of protests and petitions, secret court minutes, Alexander Solzhenitsyn's banned books, George Orwell's *Animal Farm* and *1984*, Nikolai Berdyayev's philosophical essays, documents of the Czech Spring, all sorts of sharp political discourses and angry poetry.

The impudence of the movement, even at this time of heightened persecution, reaches a point where invitations to an evening get-together include whispered lures that "a poet published by *samizdat* will be present." Of late, *samizdat* publications have percolated even into the high schools, where some of the authors and typists are the youngsters themselves. The popularity of *samizdat* with the younger generation is attested by this widely told Moscow story: A Soviet official strides into his wife's room. "Natasha, you have been typing for five straight days," he says. "*What* takes so long?" "Oh, Ivan, don't you know? I am typing

Tolstoy's *Anna Karenina*, that's what." "But why? There is the book. It's perfectly legible, you can read it in print." "Yes, but the children won't read anything unless it's typed."

The starkest paucity of illegal publications occurred in Stalin's long period between, say, 1927 and his death in 1953. His terror was too embracive to allow much, if any, underground literature. Khrushchev meant a glimpse of hope, and thus rather few people protested in the mid-fifties and early sixties. Then Khrushchev's fall in October 1964 dimmed the timid light. Still, the new Brezhnev-Kosygin terror was not so complete as Stalin's, and so underground typing and copying began to spurt in 1965–66.

The year 1965 was marked by the appearance of the clandestine journals *Russkoye slovo* (*Russian Word*), *Kolokol* (*The Bell*), both named for anti-tsarist periodicals of a century earlier, and *Sfinks* (*Sphinx*). They contained essays of sociopolitical protest, but the emphasis was mainly on free-spirited poetry.

As already noted, in September 1965 Andrei Sinyavsky and Yuli Daniel were arrested in Moscow for having published in the West, for nearly a decade, their pseudonymous antirégime books. They were tried and condemned in February 1966. The atmosphere of reaction and repression was intensified.

Nonetheless, the underground press did not abate. Instead, it shifted its accent from poetry and other literary content to politics. The protest of intellectuals against the Sinyavsky-Daniel case led to Alexander Ginzburg's *Belaya kniga* (*White Book*) of the complete minutes of the trial. In time, Ginzburg and his group—Yuri Galanskov, Aleksei Dobrovolsky, and Vera Lashkova—were also arrested and in early 1968 were tried, drawing various sentences. More than four years later, on November 4, 1972, Yuri Galanskov died in a concentration camp as a consequence of medical neglect and a bungled operation. He was then thirty-two years old, and he left behind a long, moving poem, "Chelovecheskiy manifest" ("The Human Manifesto"), with such remarkable lines as these:

Cabinet ministers, leaders, and newspapers—do not believe
  them!
Arise, you who are lying face down!

Along with his few but clarion-sounding poems, the four-
hundred-page minutes of the 1968 secret trial of Galanskov
and his group became available to *samizdat*. And it was also
in 1968 that one of the most civic-minded documents of
the underground appeared in *samizdat*: the call by Academician Andrei Sakharov, one of the fathers of the Soviet
hydrogen bomb, for progress, coexistence, and intellectual
freedom—his warning against the resurgence of Stalinism
in the Kremlin, his passionate appeal for Soviet-American
joining of hands to combat the three main catastrophes
threatening mankind: the Third World War, the planet's
pollution, and a gigantic starvation of the underprivileged
masses.

3 *Underground* Khronika

In all the spate of underground writing, only two
underground *samizdat* periodicals, issued on a regular sched-
ule, were known to survive more than for a few issues. The
more famous of the pair, *Khronika tekushchikh sobytiy*
(*Chronicle of Current Events*), began in April 1968 and
appeared every few months until the fall of 1972, when it
was finally suppressed.

The *Khronika* was strictly an information bulletin, tersely
telling its readers the news of protests and arrests of all those
nonconformist Russians, Tatars, Jews, and others; of all
those fearlessly demonstrating young scientists and engineers, lecturers and research assistants, *samizdat* writers and
distributors; and also about the latest *samizdat* publications:
what texts, on what themes, when and where, and—if
possible—the authors. Laconic yet not acerbic, the news
abounded in detail and was of many geographic origins.
Correspondents of the *Khronika* were everywhere, and the
editorial appeal to would-be volunteers was: If you have
news for our pages, give it to the person from whom you

got our bulletin, and your communication will reach us. But don't try to go up beyond that person, to the top of our ladder, lest you be taken for an informer.

The *Khronika*'s motto was Article 19 of the Universal Declaration of Human Rights, which was reproduced in each issue: "Everyone has the right to freedom of opinion and expression; this right includes freedom to hold opinions without interference and to seek, receive, and impart information through any medium and regardless of frontiers."

The good old liberal dictum (so often and mistakenly credited to Voltaire) of defending freedom of expression even for those with whom you disagree was followed by the *Khronika* editors scrupulously. The Fetisov case was an outstanding example. A Moscow economist, A. Fetisov quit the Communist Party in 1966 in protest against de-Stalinization (which, ironically enough, was just then becoming a most definite, albeit gradual, re-Stalinization).

Fetisov gathered around him three friends, all young architects, who accepted his preachment of extreme totalitarianism, chauvinism, and anti-Semitism. The group wrote and said that for 2,000 years Europe had lived in a struggle between order and disorder, and that all the time it was the Jews who were responsible for the chaos. Finally (according to the Fetisov theses), the sturdy Germanic and Slav elements rose against the Jew-caused bedlam, and this heroic effort was headed by Hitler and Stalin. The two leaders' work was a historical necessity and a positive phenomenon. But with the giant pair gone, their great contribution has been disrupted. At least in Russia it should be resumed. The Fetisov group's program recommended a deindustrialization of European Russia, a mass shift of factories and workers into Siberia, and a restoration of ancient patriarchal ways among Russian peasants. The Kremlin, alarmed by this extremism of the New Right, ordered the Fetisovists' arrest. The notorious Article 70 of the criminal code, so often used against liberals, was invoked here, too, with the result that the KGB physicians judged all four of the Fetisov group insane, and the quartet were soon under an asylum's lock and key.

A liberal *samizdat* brochure told about the whole affair

in high glee, under the title: "They Didn't Recognize Their Own Ilk." But the *Khronika* chided the brochure's authors. You must argue with those Fascists, not ridicule them, the *Khronika* said—argue calmly, objectively, scientifically. Nor should you rejoice over the imprisonment of anyone for his views, no matter how abhorrent they may be.

The *Khronika*'s lean tone led to a guess that its authors and publishers were young scientists used to dry, scholarly economy in language. Another indication of this was the *Khronika*'s regard for veracity. It constantly followed up the facts it printed; it checked them and, when needed, corrected them in subsequent issues.

The fact that the *Khronika* survived for several years suggests that new editors replaced those arrested—or even that very few were ever caught, because the editorial office was a *letuchaya redaktsiya* (literally, "editors on the fly"), with an itinerary scientifically worked out on some kind of mathematical theory of probabilities of where the police might strike next. Quite possibly, the editorship moved from one Soviet scientific center to another, then another and another —from Obninsk, say, to Dubna to Serpukhov to Novosibirsk. In the Science City (Akademgorodok) of Novosibirsk alone there were several score different research institutes. Try to find the *Khronika*'s needle in such numerous, far-flung haystacks! Yet, in late 1972, it was finally—after more than four years of thorough search—found and suppressed, its editors arrested, tried, and sentenced to slave camps and jails. In the late summer of 1973 two dissidents in particular, the historian Pyotr Yakir and the economist Viktor Levitin-Krasin, were brought to trial after a long preparation of psychological and perhaps physical pressure by their interrogators, until both were broken into confessing their role in issuing the *Khronika* and other underground literature. They were forced to "repent" publicly, and for their cooperation both were rewarded with rather mild sentences. At the same time an unsuccessful effort was made by the KGB to implicate Solzhenitsyn in the "conspiracy" of writing and publishing the *Khronika*. He was accused of at least counseling its editors.

The other long-lasting underground publication, discontinued in late 1970 or early 1971, was not known as generally as the *Khronika*. In fact, the news of its existence came after its demise and was in itself a surprise even to the most knowledgeable native and Western experts on *samizdat*. This was *Politichesky dnevnik* (*Political Diary*) which appeared in more than seventy issues from its beginning in October 1964 (the time of Khrushchev's fall) to its end in 1970 or '71. Typewritten and hand-circulated just like the *Khronika*, it was likewise uncensored, but was rather more scholarly in contents and tone. Frank but not revolutionary, the text was more of theory-discussion than of hard news, and in this it differed from *Khronika*. Unlike the wide appeal of the latter, *Politichesky dnevnik* was clearly meant for a small group of highly placed Soviet intellectuals, including quite possibly some sympathetic officials. It was its restricted character and limited circulation that made the journal relatively unknown until lately.

Indications are that *Politichesky dnevnik* was not caught and suppressed by the KGB, but that—for reasons unknown —it was terminated by its editor-publishers voluntarily.

4 *Secret Flourishes*

Had the KGB proved inept or indulgent in not repressing the *samizdat* people and publications more thoroughly? In September 1969, soon after his escape to London, the novelist Anatoly Kuznetsov declared in his letter to the American playwright Arthur Miller that "for a time, the KGB did indeed pose as a liberal cat that allowed mice to play"—so long as it did not consider the *samizdat* mice dangerous enough, and inasmuch as it knew who the mice were and where to find them if the decision to catch them was made. "Even now," wrote Kuznetsov to Miller, "the KGB does not really go after Solzhenitsyn and that kind of *samizdat*," which in Kuznetsov's opinion is not truly radically against the Soviet régime. *Samizdat* criticizes the details of the system, he insists, not the system itself. "The head of the Moscow KGB once said that he could destroy *samizdat* in two days," Kuznetsov wrote, "and this is true."

When this was quoted to another escapee, now teaching Soviet literature at the Sorbonne, the professor agreed, varying his opinion with an analogy to Mao and his hundred flowers. "You will recall," this Russian said, "that Mao encouraged those flowers of opposition to show themselves, to bloom themselves to doom. When he knew exactly the identity and whereabouts of those flowers he chopped them off."

Still another ex-Soviet academician now living in the West pointed out that the *samizdat* writers, copiers, and distributors are "a fairly narrow circle" which can easily be watched and periodically thinned. "This is precisely what the KGB is doing," he said, "but while constantly pruned, or even stunted, the tree of the opposition can still be useful to the régime as a kind of safety valve, if I may mix a metaphor or two. *Samizdat* is deliberately allowed to exist to prevent a far worse explosion of anti-Soviet feeling." Some of the *samizdat* items may, in fact, even be originated by the KGB, he went on, either as bait for some poor suspected fish in the underground stream or, in the larger policy, as a general safety valve.

The KGB works with deadly efficiency mostly when it deals with organizations. But *samizdat* often baffles the KGB because the *samizdat* network is nebulous. The *samizdat* people relate to one another in a loose, chummy way, either as office mates or as friends dropping in at one another's houses in the evening or at *dachas* for weekends of much tea and endless talk. Once they feel one another out and are sure, they enter the phase of complete mutual trust.

This is where *samizdat* begins—and still there seldom is any definite organization. The first four or eight copies of the original typing quickly disappear—and most if not all of these copies produce their own four or eight copies each. The geometric progression is thus on its way. Can KGB track down all those countless copies and their readers, copiers, and distributors? "Absolutely impossible," say those who know. "The authors and copiers just melt away."

5 Typewriter as Weapon

The capture of a regular printing press rather than a typewriter has been mentioned by the secret police on rare occasions. Once, years back, the KGB reported finding a printing press run by Jehovah's Witnesses in a Ukrainian cellar. Another time, in 1969, a printing press was seized together with a group of naval officers, serving with an atomic submarine berthed in Tallinn, Estonia, who were using the press for their *samizdat* literature.

Office duplicators are scarce in the Soviet Union. Private ownership of them is prohibited. Mostly, they are in research institutes, and the KGB watches each machine with top-priority zeal. Yet duplicating does occur. And there is at least one known case of microfilm's large-scale use: The typescript of the several hundred pages of Zhores A. Medvedev's *The Rise and Fall of T. D. Lysenko,* banned by the Soviet government and circulating for some time in *samizdat,* was finally reduced to a microfilm and sent to the United States where an English translation was eventually published by the Columbia University Press.

Typewriters are hard to trace in the Soviet Union because only a few brands are in use, and there are countless thousands of each of these exactly alike. A unique impression made by a certain letter of an individual typewriter can be tracked only through an original page and perhaps its first carbon copy. The KGB's difficulty is compounded by the *samizdat* practice of dividing a manuscript among several typists at once, for speed and conspiracy both.

Some editors deliberately open the gate to *samizdat* when they know that a certain submitted manuscript will not be passed by the censors. The editor will send out copies of the manuscript to, say, fifteen regular consultants of his publishing house for their opinion. All fifteen reply, "Sorry, it's too dangerous to be published," but at least one of them (if not more) lets *samizdat* people copy the manuscript before he returns it.

Even a few cases of KGB officers showing unexpected leniency have been reported. One secret policeman concluded his search of a *samizdat* fan's premises by saying: "This item is quite harmless, so I will confiscate it, but this one is really important—take it back and hide it well." In another case a girl student was busy typing certain religious-philosophical works at night. Finally caught, her typewriter taken, she was told to be ready for a solemn Party meeting at her school during which she would be officially castigated and possibly expelled. The KGB man said: "You will hear from the chairman of your Party unit when and where to appear." "But," said the girl, "I am the chairman." The man emitted a startled laugh, and, after a moment's thought, decided: "All right, then, never mind. Just be more careful in the future." And returned the typewriter to her. A Soviet Russian dissident commented: "Such minor officers feel, as we say, 'more at home with their souls' when they all of a sudden go soft on their quarry."

6 Westward Exportation

Much of *samizdat* is sent abroad, for reprinting and return to the USSR and for translation—for the world to know. Wherever advisable, the Russian émigré editors and publishers append a note: "This came to us from the Soviet Union without the author's knowledge. We print it without his permission." Which may indeed ease the author's fate if he is arrested, but does not absolve him entirely.

Five Russian émigré periodicals regularly publish the latest from *samizdat*: in Frankfurt, the monthly *Posev* (*Sowing*) and the quarterly *Grani* (*Frontiers*); in Paris, the weekly *Russkaya mysl'* (*Russian Thought*); and in New York, the daily *Novoye russkoye slovo* (*New Russian Word*) and the quarterly *Novy zhurnal* (*New Review*). There are also several publishing houses, Russian and non-Russian, in Western Europe and the United States specializing in *samizdat*. The whole is known among Soviet readers as *tamizdat*, a Russian word of later coinage and less spread than *samizdat*. It refers to printed (not typed) material smuggled into the USSR from outside; the first three letters, *tam*, mean "over there"—in this case the West.

Another Western group that has come to notice for its contacts with *samizdat* is the Alexander Herzen Foundation of Amsterdam. Named in honor of the famous Russian émigré who a century ago, in London, published his *Kolokol* for smuggling into tsarist Russia, the foundation is run by two Dutchmen and one Englishman: Karel van het Reve and Jan Bezemer, both professors of Russian literature and both former newspaper correspondents in Moscow, and Peter Reddaway, a lecturer at the London School of Economics. Its program is to publish "quickly and responsibly manuscripts written in the USSR which cannot be published there because of censorship." It stands for freedom of expression in works "of literary or documentary value, irrespective of their political, philosophical, or religious tendency, and with the minimum of editing." The aim is to publish manuscripts from Russia first in Russian, to safeguard copyright for the authors and for possible smuggling back into the USSR, and then in translation by whichever good Western publisher may be interested.

In New York a group of Americans, both native and of Russian origin, operates a publishing house formerly called Inter-Language Literary Associates, but more recently renamed the Chekhov Publishing House, whose reprints of Osip Mandelshtam's poetry and other such banned-in-Russia works find their way into the USSR. In Rome and Paris, two loosely related groups of Americans and some French-born Russians maintain remarkable contacts with such Russian readers. The Paris group, known as the IMKA Press, emphasizes religious and philosophical publications, but it is also responsible for bringing out of the USSR and publishing in the West some of Mikhail Bulgakov's writings still banned by the Soviet government. In 1971, when that government prohibited Solzhenitsyn's *August 1914*, he arranged for this Paris organization to publish its Russian text. In late 1973 he chose the IMKA Press also for the first Western publication of his forbidden *The Gulag Archipelago*.

Last but not least, there is the *radizdat*—the broadcasting of many of the *samizdat* protests, petitions, brochures, and whole books to the Soviet Union by such outlets as Radio Liberty in Munich. A degree of American governmental aid for all or much of this effort is generally reported to be a fact. "Why not?" Western pragmatists ask. "If Moscow finances so much of Communist propaganda the world over, why shouldn't Washington aid at least *tamizdat* and *radizdat*, if not *samizdat* directly?"

That the efforts of the *tamizdat* activists is appreciated may be seen from the eagerness with which its publications are sought out by Soviet readers. Since the long-ago Khrushchevian promise of republishing Mandelshtam's poetry was not kept for more than a decade, and when finally printed in late 1973 the 30,000 copies of the pressrun were quickly bought up, the demand for this tragic poetry is high, and the Western three-volume edition of his work (issued in Russian in New York) goes on the black market of Moscow and other cities for two hundred rubles (some $275 at the official Soviet rate in these mid-1970s).

But those caught importing, selling, or buying such forbidden books are arrested and receive stiff jail or slave-camp sentences. Penalties depend on the authors. Works by Solzhenitsyn are feared by the Communist leadership more than those by Andrei Sakharov, the physicist who in recent years has authored bold memoranda warning Brezhnev and his associates against their neo-Stalinism and urging them to usher in a new sane foreign and domestic policy. As one wise Soviet nonconformist has remarked, "Solzhenitsyn's admirers and readers in his homeland are regarded by the Kremlin as mystics, easily swept and multiplied by his influence, but Sakharov and other nonconformist scientists are considered by Brezhnev as too rational to appeal broadly to the average Russian mind." And so, KGB sentences for dealing in the Solzhenitsyn and Sakharov *samizdat* and *tamizdat* are meted out accordingly.

In 1973–74, after joining the international copyright agreement, the Soviet government tried using it to intimidate Solzhenitsyn and other *samizdat* writers against the continued relay of their manuscripts out of the country for

publication in the West, and even to threaten Western
publishers with legal action in Western courts if these
houses persisted in publishing such forbidden Russian authors, the copyright for whose work, the Kremlin claimed,
belonged not to these writers but to the Soviet state. So far
such attempts at intimidation and such threats of court
action have been fruitless.

Exactly how does the fabulous *samizdat* literature of
Soviet nonconformists run its underground routes Westward? And how does it, transformed into the West-printed
tamizdat and West-originated *radizdat* broadcasts, return to
an ever widening audience in the Soviet Union?

For mailing, telegraphing, telephoning, or transporting
samizdat material Westward, foreign correspondents in Moscow were until lately a much used medium. They still accept
from the dissidents their rebellious and newsy petitions,
protests, and mini-manifestos. But with so many nonconformists recently arrested or given their visas to New York,
Paris, Vienna, Rome, or Tel Aviv, the river of such material
gradually is becoming a rivulet. And less willingly than
formerly do the foreign journalists accept for relay to the
West bulky *samizdat* manuscripts of novels or polemics.

The reason is the increasing KGB pressure on such resi-
dent foreigners to cease their ties with the native rebels. Ex-
pulsions of correspondents or non-granting of return visas
to them have grown more frequent. Accepting from the dissidents those weighty envelopes with many pages is now
rather dangerous. Mailing or taking them to the West by
foreigners is too involved a matter.

The role of diplomatic personnel in Moscow as *samizdat*'s
transmission belt to foreign lands is necessarily misty. Yet
in these 1970s diplomatic pouches out of Moscow are uti-
lized by *samizdat* activists, even if with extreme care. An
attaché, a secretary, a courier is used once, and no more.
Repeated use of the same messenger is out of the question.
The KGB, with all its cleverness, is hard put to guess which
of the embassies may be the next channel. If any pouch is
interfered with by the KGB, and no *samizdat* contraband is
found, foreign governments may protest vigorously.

Ordinary tourists are sometimes used to bring illegal

literature from and into the Soviet Union. Russian sailors of the tremendously expanded Soviet merchant marine are ingenious and often successful carriers of this kind of contraband among others.

Plain mail is frequently used by people sending *samizdat* items out of the Soviet Union and *tamizdat* literature being sent into that country. The names and addresses of the recipients are correct, but return names and addresses are of course invented. The intended recipients within the Soviet Union, if the subversive mail is intercepted by the Soviet secret police, protest angrily that they neither know the senders nor have ever asked for such horrible literature. If the addressees live abroad, they merely miss the confiscated packages. But many items do slip through the KGB net. The volume of all categories of mail in the Soviet Union is so great by now that the censors cannot physically check it all. There is spot-checking only; a hit-and-miss affair, really, not at all scientifically devised.

One interesting category of eager volunteers sending or smuggling *samizdat* to foreign lands was until lately the kind of people who wanted to "help Solzhenitsyn." But Solzhenitsyn was far from pleased. His work, as circulated by typing copyists, was often—even if unintentionally—distorted in the very process of *samizdat* copying. Through his public protest and personal correspondence with his own foreign contacts however, he established a rigorous control of his writing as it was published abroad.

Part of Solzhenitsyn's past difficulty in preserving the purity of his texts and the choice of his foreign publishers came from the fact that "helping Solzhenitsyn" had become a matter of status among his admirers in the homeland. Some Soviet readers sent him money, and quite a few even liked to boast of it. Others wanted to help or merely seek status by insisting on mailing *samizdat* texts by Solzhenitsyn to foreign addresses without the author's consent and whether or not such items were already known abroad. In several instances Solzhenitsyn, irritated by such unsolicited aid and even suspicious of the motives or connections of such "well-wishers," firmly showed them to the door.

What were Solzhenitsyn's own methods of safeguarding

his manuscripts from those unwanted admirers and relaying his writings to his Western publishers despite the multi-headed Cerberus of the KGB? What were the mechanics of this amazing flow of freedom's dream?

Solzhenitsyn and his friends have revealed that he sent his later manuscripts, beginning with *August 1914*, to Dr. Fritz Heeb, the well-known Swiss lawyer with international literary connections, who then arranged for publication in Russian by the IMKA Press in Paris, and in other languages by prominent publishing houses the world over. The colorful activists of the IMKA Press, Russians born or growing up in France, hadn't met Solzhenitsyn before they brought out such books as his *August 1914* and *The Gulag Archipelago*, but he trusted them completely. And they returned his faith in them by treating his texts with reverence and utter care.

Even Dr. Heeb hadn't met or even spoken on the telephone with Solzhenitsyn until his expulsion from Russia in 1974. After Dr. Heeb had concluded his first agreement with the writer, the Swiss lawyer waited nearly a year before the manuscript of *August 1914* finally reached him: not only was the author still polishing his work, but also he and his Soviet friends and aides were painstakingly cautious in relaying the manuscript to Switzerland.

The exact method of delivery cannot be divulged, obviously. But several sound guesses may be made. In Solzhenitsyn's case the most natural way would be by sending his manuscripts and letters via his connections in the music and theater world. High-ranking Soviet performers going on tours of the West can easily bring practically anything from and to the USSR without the KGB inspection and detection, simply because such élite have *spravki*, the plural of *spravka*, a prized certificate from the Soviet authorities exempting its holder from any KGB search at airports and other control points. But now, much as he disliked being pitched out of his beloved Russia, Solzhenitsyn can write as he pleases and, relieved of financial burdens, he can concentrate more freely on his fictional and nonfictional writings.

7   *Tape Recorder as Weapon*

Inside the Soviet Union there is also a musical *samizdat*: Russian songs circulating on tape, of sly or outright antirégime nature, sung to the accompaniment of guitars. Sometimes it is also called *magnitizdat*, from *magnitnaya lenta*, the two Russian words for tape used in tape recorders. The already mentioned Bulat Okudzhava, the popular and talented poet-minstrel, began the trend in the 1950s and, despite governmental frowns and threats, the mode caught on. Okudzhava's lyrics were subtly bitter-humorous and fostered dissent without openly calling for a revolt. The singers that have followed him are funnier and folksier, acrid and devil-may-care. In the 1970s, anti-bureaucracy songs, concentration-camp ballads, rough-melodic protests of the have-nots against the Soviet haves, are their main repertory. Along with the tapes of the songs, *samizdat* transcripts of the lyrics are secretly available.

Alexander Galich and Vladimir Vysotsky are the foremost bards of this *magnitizdat*. Galich is the better known of the two. Born in 1919 (real name Ginzburg), he started his career as an actor in the Stanislavsky School and during the Second World War was a member of a theatrical company playing to soldier audiences at the front. Becoming a playwright, he saw ten of his plays staged, but three of his best were not allowed for production. In December 1971 he was expelled from the Union of Soviet Writers, and later subjected to other persecution, on charges of pro-Westernism and other activities as a dissident. He began his antirégime singing when he was nearly fifty. In one of his most famous songs, in praise of the literary *samizdat*, he sings of a typewriter named Erika.

> *Erika makes four copies,*
> *Not much, but enough.*
> *For the time being let there be only four copies,*
> *It's really enough!*

This one is a great subversive hit in the Soviet Union. If any song can be called the hymn of *samizdat*, this is it. By his boldness, Galich practically claims legality. In fact, most openly, Galich is one of the founder-members of what its creators insist is a perfectly legitimate organization of Soviet dissent. In June 1974 he was finally allowed to leave for West Europe.

8   The Force of Continued Protest

The Committee on Human Rights was formed by Sakharov and several of his scientist friends in November 1970 to uphold and defend liberties as spelled out in both the Soviet constitution and various United Nations documents. Soon Solzhenitsyn joined it. In June 1971 the Committee formally affiliated itself with the International League for the Rights of Man, whose headquarters are in New York.

In the reality of the Soviet Union this Committee was a fearless step, an astounding novelty, since for decades no committee or any other organization had been allowed by the Communist Party to exist and function unless established by that Party. The Committee on Human Rights insisted that it was not a political organization and thus not anti-Soviet. Its by-laws proclaimed that no member of any political party could be a member of the Committee. Yet, since the only party in the Soviet Union is the Communist Party, this means that no Communist could join this Committee on Human Rights—a daring statement, indeed.

A particularly active member of the Committee was Dr. Valery N. Chalidze, a prominent Soviet physicist. The KGB repeatedly searched his apartment; went through and confiscated his files of writings, his own and others'; threatened and harassed him, but he and his colleagues stubbornly continued with their cause.

In his cramped lodgings Chalidze published the typewritten *Obshchestvennyie problemy* (*Social Problems*). Issued as a bimonthly since October 1969, it was a *samizdat* journal with a difference. Unlike *Khronika* or any other less known periodical or book or brochure in the underground, it was a fearlessly open magazine, with Chalidze's name and address clearly typed on its pages, and the Committee's name and aims boldly spelled out. It was devoted almost exclusively to legal problems in the broad field of human rights. In and out of the magazine pages Chalidze and his associates came to the public and articulate aid of a number of Soviet citizens arrested on charges of typing, distributing, or simply reading *samizdat* publications. Among such cases the Committee declared its concern for the fate of Revol't Pimenov, a Leningrad mathematician arrested and tried in October 1970 for keeping and reading *samizdat* publications. The Communist official who interrogated Pimenov on these charges voiced the Party's attitude toward the Committee on Human Rights when he said to Pimenov: "Your scientific achievements are well and good. But we do still have enough power. Never will there be any concessions at all in the sphere of ideology!" Pimenov was convicted and sent off to five years of Siberian exile. Still, the Committee and men and women like Pimenov went on with their implacable will to freedom, their struggle for human rights.

In the early 1970s a new and rather effective method of combating the dissidents was decided upon by the Communist rulers: While continuing arrests and sentencing of many of them, get rid of certain leaders of the movement by letting them go to the Western countries and not allowing them to return to the Soviet Union. Thus will the movement be deprived of its most energetic and fearless firebrands.

And so, in 1972, the Soviet government permitted Chalidze to leave for the United States for a series of lectures at American universities. In December, agents of the Soviet embassy in Washington traveled to New York—to retrieve the Soviet passports of Dr. Chalidze and his wife (a descendant of the famous revolutionary and Soviet commissar of foreign affairs, Maxim Litvinov). Cancellation of their Soviet citizenship followed.

A similar course of action was taken in 1973 against another celebrated dissident, the Soviet scientist Zhores Medvedev. His passport was taken away from him after he had been allowed to go to England, and he was deprived of Soviet citizenship. Other dissidents were given their visas to leave the Soviet Union for good; among them the poet Iosif Brodsky and the mathematician-poet Alexander Yesenin-Volpe (Sergei Yesenin's son), both of whom are now émigrés teaching on American campuses.

But many more of the ardent latter-day nonconformists are not permitted to leave. They are sent to prisons, to concentration camps, and, worst of all, to insane asylums—despite their perfect sanity, now being relentlessly pushed on the road to insanity through injections of special drugs. An outstanding case is that of the young historian Andrei Amalrik, who for his several books of protest and uncomfortable prophecy of the Soviet Union's eventual doom and breakdown has over the course of several recent years been repeatedly punished by arrests, imprisonment, and hard menial labor in exile in Northeastern Siberia. Another striking instance is that of General Pyotr Grigorenko, a bemedaled hero of the Second World War, who for his brave dissidence by writing and speaking out was sent to a Soviet mental institution. (Finally released in July 1974.)

And yet, the protest continues, particularly by writers. The question arises: Where does all this amazing nonconformism and active dissent come from? Much of the answer is that the thirst for freedom has always been there; that it survived through the entire Soviet period against all the odds, and at least in part through the oligarchs' own mistaken actions; that the roots of dissidence go far back, are deep and wondrous and simply cannot be stamped out. This is one of the points which should be made to prove that Russia's so-called age-old tradition of submission to autocracy and ignorance is never the whole truth of the matter.

From the very beginning of the Soviet era, the works of Alexander Pushkin, Mikhail Lermontov, Nikolai Gogol, Ivan Turgenev, Lev Tolstoy, Anton Chekhov, and even some of the novels of Fyodor Dostoyevsky (but not *The Possessed* which so clairvoyantly predicted the inhumanity of revolutionaries), were reprinted by the Soviet government in numerous editions. So were certain novels of Western classics. But as these Russian and foreign classics were given to the Soviet reader and student, special "class struggle" prefaces were appended to "explain" and thus dehumanize the noble texts.

Soviet leaders must have all along realized that all such Soviet prefaces and Red classroom lectures could not outweigh the humanistic, liberty-loving message of those durable books. But so intent were the new autocrats on proving that they, too, appreciated culture, and so resolved were they to parade as the true inheritors and natural continuators of all the good in old Russia, that they took the risk of opening floodgates of free thought as they reprinted the classics in editions larger than ever.

And still, the appreciation and practice of true culture and the desire for real freedom defy the governmental effort to "explain away" Russian classics and the Kremlin's fiat to hate and deride the best there is in Western philosophy, art, and literature. Found among the genuine intelligentsia on levels below the Brezhnev-Kosygin commanding heights, this quest for culture and this longing for liberty are pro-Western in the sense that a great deal of old prerevolutionary Russian culture owed its strength to Western patterns. In much of its semisecret credo today, in many of its practices open or not, this culture stems from the best that was in Russia's civilization prior to November 1917.

And so this seeking, this appreciation, did continue amid the official Soviet aridity and primitivism which only yesterday seemed to be slaying forever any such comprehension of truth, beauty, and freedom. For the historical fact is that the Lenin-Stalin destruction of old meanings in the culture and liberty of Russia was never complete, despite the two dictators' clear intent to wipe these out thoroughly. The Communists in Russia killed off entire classes, but individuals and influences of those classes inevitably survived. The Communists attempted to use old culture and its riches for their own ends, but the spirit of that old freedom-loving, freedom-preaching culture would neither be bent nor wastefully spent.

As late as the 1930s, through the bleakest time of the purges, there remained in Russia the so-called "inner émigrés," men and women of the prerevolutionary intelligentsia who either refused, or did not manage, to flee abroad while escape was yet possible. They lived on in the Soviet Union, making a mere surface compromise between their own and the Soviet ideas of verity and beauty. They paid lip service to the new yet retrograde Soviet premises in politics and arts, but in their own tight family circles and even sometimes among their few trusted friends they kept alive their own beloved values of Western and old Russian civilization.

Importantly, they succeeded in relaying some of this precious heritage to their progeny, and in rare but unmistakable cases also to some strangers—to the new intellectuals rising from the peasant and worker masses. But this last group, the new Soviet intelligentsia of lower-class origin, apparently did not need much if any teaching from the surviving old intellectuals. The old culture which Soviet propagandists tried to use for their reactionary ends, but which stubbornly resisted such usage, was itself the teacher of the new intelligentsia.

Such were the well-hidden seed-beds of whatever genuine green shoots of old-Russia-rooted, West-inspired culture and freedom we now see among some Soviet intellectuals. True, these restless, questing writers, artists, students, scientists, and engineers are a mere handful, seemingly lost among the Soviet conformers and suppressors. Their understanding of the West is at times but a feeble shadow of the old Russian intelligentsia's full-blooded borrowing from, and improvement upon, the West. And only very recently, since the middle and late 1950s, and particularly since the 1960s, have their writers come forth to continue the gifts and traditions of Tolstoy, Dostoyevsky, and Chekhov.

It is generally agreed that by now, through KGB repression, open dissidence may be somewhat dwindling and that even the Sakharov-Maksimov-Solzhenitsyn-Galich Committee on Human Rights is dying or dormant, but that *samizdat*, by its very nature, is far from ebbing. The 1967 prediction by Georgy Vladimov (writing under his *samizdat* pen name of Volosevich) addressed to the powers that be of the Fourth Congress of the Union of Soviet Writers has proved to be valid: "Do spring those mass-scale searches of yours, do arrest the *samizdat* authors and distributors. At least one copy will escape undetected—and will multiply, in a yet greater abundance, at that."

The significant fact nonetheless persists that there are such new writers and other intellectuals in the Soviet Union, and that they are growing in depth, stature, and daring. Already in the 1950s Pasternak and Dudintsev were signs of the new times, while in the 1960s the light burned yet more brightly with Sinyavsky and Daniel. And in the 1970s Solzhenitsyn and the protest of *samizdat* were unbowed and Solzhenitsyn had, by his boldness and his talent, so effectively captured the admiration and respect of the world that his oppressors didn't dare to harm him, and could only send him into exile, where he continues his literary activity.

And now, new writers are making their impact in Russia because they bring with them the civic courage and other sterling values of the unforgotten prerevolutionary past of nonconformity and defiance.

Suggested Readings

For whatever English translations may be available of the titles mentioned in this book, the reader is to consult the catalogue or the reference librarian of the nearest large city or university library.

In addition, the following biographical and critical studies are suggested (only books are included; essays and articles, as being far too numerous, are omitted).

Literature: General (also Groups and Movements)

Alexandrova, Vera. *A History of Soviet Literature, 1917–1962.* Translated by Mirra Ginsburg. Garden City, N.Y.: Doubleday, 1963.

Bowra, C. M. *Poetry and Politics, 1900–1960.* Cambridge: Cambridge University Press, 1966.

Brown, Edward J. *The Proletarian Episode in Russian Literature, 1928–1932.* New York: Columbia University Press, 1953. Reprint. New York: Octagon, 1971.

———. *Russian Literature Since the Revolution.* Revised edition. New York: Collier Books, 1969.

Carlisle, Olga Andreyev. *Voices in the Snow: Encounters with Russian Writers.* New York: Random House, 1962.

Eastman, Max. *Artists in Uniform: A Study of Literature and Bureaucratism.* New York: Alfred A. Knopf, 1934.

Field, Andrew, ed. *Pages from Tarussa, New Voices in Russian Writing.* London: Chapman and Hall, 1964.

Gibian, George. *Interval of Freedom: Soviet Literature During the Thaw, 1954–1957.* Minneapolis: University of Minnesota Press, 1960.

————, ed. and trans. *Russia's Lost Literature of the Absurd. A Literary Discovery. Selected Works of Daniil Kharms and Alexander Vvedensky.* Ithaca: Cornell University Press, 1971.

Hayward, Max, and Labedz, Leopold, eds. *Literature and Revolution in Soviet Russia, 1917–1962.* New York: Oxford University Press, 1963.

Holthusen, Johannes. *Twentieth-Century Russian Literature: A Critical Study.* Translated from the German by Theodore Huebener. New York: Frederick Ungar, 1972.

Johnson, Priscilla. *Khrushchev and the Arts: The Politics of Soviet Culture, 1962–1964.* Cambridge, Mass.: Massachusetts Institute of Technology Press, 1965.

London, Kurt. *The Seven Soviet Arts.* 1937. Reprint. Westport, Conn.: Greenwood Press, 1970.

Maguire, Robert A. *Red Virgin Soil: Soviet Literature in the 1920's.* Princeton: Princeton University Press, 1968.

Markov, Vladimir. *Russian Futurism: A History.* Berkeley: University of California Press, 1968.

————, and Sparks, Merrill, eds. *Modern Russian Poetry: An Anthology with Verse Translations.* Indianapolis: Bobbs-Merrill, 1966.

Matejka, Ladislav, and Pomorska, Krystyna, eds. *Readings in Russian Poetics: Formalist and Structuralist Views.* Cambridge, Mass., and London: Massachusetts Institute of Technology Press, 1971.

Mihailovich, Vasa D., comp. and ed. *Modern Slavic Literatures.* Vol. 1: *Russian Literature.* New York: Frederick Ungar, 1972.

Morton, Miriam, ed. Foreward to *A Harvest of Russian Children's Literature,* by Ruth Hill Vigeurs. Berkeley and Los Angeles: University of California Press, 1967.

Muchnic, Helen. *From Gorky to Pasternak: Six Writers in Soviet Russia.* New York: Random House, 1961.

Oulanoff, Hongor. *The Serapion Brothers: Theory and Practice.* The Hague: Mouton, 1966.

Poggioli, Renato. *The Poets of Russia, 1890–1930.* Cambridge: Harvard University Press, 1960.

Proffer, Carl R., and Proffer, Ellendea, eds. *Russian Literature Triquarterly.* Ann Arbor: Ardis Publishers, beginning with Number 1, Fall 1971.

Reavey, George, ed. and trans. *The New Russian Poets 1953–1966: An Anthology.* New York: October House, 1966.

Reilly, Alayne P. *America in Contemporary Soviet Literature.* New York: New York University Press, 1971.

Rühle, Jürgen, *Literature and Revolution: A Critical Study of the Writer and Communism in the Twentieth Century*. Translated and edited by Jean Steinberg. New York: Praeger, 1969.

Siegel, Paul N., ed. *Leon Trotsky on Literature and Art*. New York: Pathfinder Press, 1970.

Slonim, Marc. *An Outline of Russian Literature*. New York: Oxford University Press, 1958.

———. *Soviet Russian Literature*. New York: Oxford University Press, 1964.

———. *Soviet Russian Literature: Writers and Problems, 1917–1967*. Revised edition. New York: Oxford University Press, 1967.

Struve, Gleb. *Russian Literature Under Lenin and Stalin, 1917–1953*. Norman: University of Oklahoma Press, 1971.

Thompson, Ewa M. *Russian Formalism and Anglo-American New Criticism: A Comparative Study*. The Hague: Mouton, 1971.

Thomson, Boris. *The Premature Revolution: Russian Literature and Society, 1917–1946*. London: Weidenfeld and Nicolson, 1972.

Vickery, Walter N. *The Cult of Optimism: Political and Ideological Problems of Recent Soviet Literature*. Bloomington: Indiana University Press, 1963.

Whitney, Thomas P., ed. *The New Writing in Russia*. Ann Arbor: The University of Michigan Press, 1964.

Williams, Robert C. *Culture in Exile: Russian Emigrés in Germany, 1881–1941*. Ithaca: Cornell University Press, 1972.

Yarmolinsky, Avrahm. *Literature Under Communism: The Literary Policy of the Communist Party of the Soviet Union from the End of World War II to the Death of Stalin*. Bloomington: Indiana University Publications, 1960.

Zavalishin, Viacheslav. *Early Soviet Writers*. New York: Praeger, 1958.

Literature: Individual Authors

AKHMATOVA

Driver, Sam N. *Anna Akhmatova*. New York: Twayne Publishers, 1972.

Verheul, Kees. *The Theme of Time in the Poetry of Anna Axmatova*. The Hague: Mouton, 1971.

ANDREYEV

Kaun, Alexander. *Leonid Andreyev: A Critical Study*. New York: Huebsch, 1924.

Newcombe, Josephine M. *Leonid Andreyev*. New York: Frederick Ungar, 1973.

Woodward, James B. *Lenoid Andreyev: A Study*. Oxford: Clarendon Press, 1969.

BABEL

Babel, Nathalie, ed. *Isaac Babel: The Lonely Years, 1925–1959*. New York: Farrar, Straus and Co., Inc., 1964.

Carden, Patricia. *The Art of Isaac Babel*. Ithaca: Cornell University Press, 1972.

Hallett, Richard. *Isaac Babel*. New York: Frederick Ungar, 1973.

BLOK

Vogel, Lucy E. *Aleksandr Blok: The Journey to Italy*. Ithaca: Cornell University Press, 1973.

CHEKHOV

Avilov, Lydia. *Chekhov in My Life*. Translated with an introduction by David Magarshack. New York: Harcourt, Brace and Co., 1950.

Jackson, Robert L. *Chekhov: A Collection of Critical Essays*. Englewood Cliffs, N.J.: Prentice-Hall, 1967.

Karlinsky, Simon, ed. *Letters of Anton Chekhov*. New York: Harper & Row, 1973.

Magarshack, David. *Chekhov: A Life*. New York: Grove Press, 1952.

Melchinger, Siegfried. *Anton Chekhov*. Translated by Edith Tarcov. New York: Frederick Ungar, 1972.

Simmons, Ernest J. *Chekhov: A Biography*. Boston: Little, Brown and Co., 1962.

GORKY

Borras, F. M. *Maxim Gorky the Writer: An Interpretation*. Oxford: Clarendon Press, 1967.

Kaun, Alexander. *Maxim Gorky and His Russia*. New York: Jonathan Cape & Harrison Smith, 1931.

Weil, Irwin. *Gorky: His Literary Development and Influence on Soviet Intellectual Life.* New York: Random House, 1966.

Wolfe, Bertram D. *The Bridge and the Abyss: The Troubled Friendship of Maxim Gorky and V. I. Lenin.* New York: Praeger, 1967.

Yershov, Peter, ed. *Letters of Gorky and Andreyev, 1899–1912.* New York: Columbia University Press, 1958.

(Although it is a work of fiction, Igor Gouzenko's *The Fall of a Titan* [translated by Mervyn Black; New York: Norton, 1954], tells some of the factual story of Gorky's poisoning on Stalin's orders. Gouzenko, a former member of the Soviet secret service, undoubtedly had access to facts. It is a pity that he chose to fictionalize what he knew of Gorky's death.)

HIPPIUS (Gippius)

Matich, Olga. *Paradox in the Religious Poetry of Zinaida Gippius.* Munich: Wilhelm Fink, 1972.

Pachmuss, Temira. *Zinaida Hippius: An Intellectual Profile.* Carbondale and Edwardsville: Southern Illinois University Press, 1971.

KAVERIN

Piper, D. G. B. *V. A. Kaverin: A Soviet Writer's Response to the Problem of Commitment: The Relationship of Skandalist and Khudozhnik Neizvesten to the Development of Soviet Literature in the Late Nineteen-Twenties.* Pittsburgh: Duquesne University Press, 1970.

MANDELSHTAM

Brown, Clarence. *Mandelstam.* New York: Cambridge University Press, 1973.

Mandelstam, Nadezhda. *Hope Against Hope: A Memoir.* Translated by Max Hayward. New York: Atheneum, 1970.

———. *Hope Abandoned.* Translated by Max Hayward. New York: Atheneum, 1973.

MAYAKOVSKY

Brown, Edward J. *Mayakovsky: A Poet in the Revolution.* Princeton: Princeton University Press, 1973.

Humesky, Assaya. *Majakovskij and His Neologisms.* New York: Rausen, 1966.

Shklovsky, Viktor. *Mayakovsky and His Circle*. Edited and translated by Lily Feiler. New York: Dodd, Mead & Co., 1972.

Stahlberger, Lawrence L. *The Symbolic System of Mayakovsky*. The Hague: Mouton, 1966.

NABOKOV

Dembo, L. S., ed. *Nabokov: The Man and His Work*. Madison: University of Wisconsin Press, 1967.

Field, Andrew. *Nabokov: His Life in Art, A Critical Narrative*. Boston: Little, Brown and Co., 1967.

OLESHA

Beaujour, Elizabeth Klosty. *The Invisible Land: A Study of the Artistic Imagination of Iurii Olesha*. New York and London: Columbia University Press, 1970.

PASTERNAK

Dyck, J. W. *Boris Pasternak*. New York: Twayne Publishers, 1972.

Plank, Dale L. *Pasternak's Lyric: A Study of Sound and Imagery*. The Hague: Mouton, 1966.

Rowland, Mary F., and Rowland, Paul. Preface to *Pasternak's Doctor Zhivago*, by Harry T. Moore. Carbondale and Edwardsville: Southern Illinois University Press, 1967.

Ruge, Gerd. *Pasternak: A Pictorial Biography*. New York: McGraw-Hill Book Co., Inc., 1959.

SHOLOKHOV

Stewart, D. H. *Mikhail Sholokhov: A Critical Introduction*. Ann Arbor: University of Michigan Press, 1967.

SINYAVSKY and DANIEL

Hayward, Max, ed. *On Trial: The Soviet State Versus "Abram Tertz" and "Nikolai Arzhak."* New York: Harper & Row, 1966.

SOLZHENITSYN

Björkegren, Hans. *Aleksandr Solzhenitsyn: A Biography*. Translated by Kaarina Eneberg, New York: The Third Press, Joseph Okpaku Publishing Co., 1972.

176   SUGGESTED READINGS

Burg, David, and Feifer, George. *Solzhenitsyn*. New York: Stein and Day, 1972.

Dunlop, John B., Haugh, Richard, and Klimoff, Alexis, eds. *Aleksandr Solzhenitsyn: Critical Essays and Documentary Materials*. Belmont, Mass.: Nordland Publishing Co., 1973.

Fiene, Donald M., comp. *Alexander Solzhenitsyn: An International Bibliography of Writings By and About Him*. Ann Arbor: Ardis Publishers, 1973.

Labedz, Leopold, ed. Foreword to *Solzhenitsyn: A Documentary Record*, by Harrison E. Salisbury. New York: Harper & Row, 1971.

Lukacs, Georg. *Solzhenitsyn*. Translated by William David Graf. Cambridge, Mass: Massachusetts Institute of Technology Press, 1971.

Medvedev, Zhores. *Ten Years After Ivan Denisovich*. Translated from the Russian by Hilary Sternberg. New York: Alfred A. Knopf, 1973.

Rothberg, Abraham. *Aleksandr Solzhenitsyn—The Major Novels*. Ithaca: Cornell University Press, 1971.

TSVETAYEVA

Karlinsky, Simon. *Marina Cvetaeva* [Tsvetayeva]: *Her Art and Life*. Berkeley: University of California Press, 1966.

YESENIN

de Graaff, Frances. *Sergej Esenin: A Biographical Sketch*. The Hague: Mouton, 1966.

Theater and Films

Barna, Yon. Foreword to *Eisenstein* by Jay Leyda. Bloomington: Indiana University Press, 1974.

Bowers, Faubion. *Broadway, U.S.S.R.: Ballet, Theatre, and Entertainment in Russia Today*. New York: Thomas Nelson & Sons, 1959.

Carter, Huntly. *The New Spirit in the Russian Theatre, 1917–1928*. 1929. Reprint. New York: Arno, 1970.

———. *The New Theatre and Cinema of Soviet Russia*. 1924. Reprint. New York: Arno, 1970.

Cowell, Raymond, ed. *Twelve Modern Dramatists*. Oxford: Pergamon Press, 1967.

Leyda, Jay. *Kino: A History of the Russian and Soviet Film*.

New York: Macmillan, 1960; reprint, Collier Books, 1973.

Magarshack, David. *Stanislavsky: A Life*. London: MacGibbon & Kee, 1950.

Moore, Sonia. *The Stanislavsky Method: the Professional Training of an Actor*. New York: Viking Press, 1960.

Styan, J. L. *Chekhov in Performance: A Commentary on the Major Plays*. Cambridge and New York: Cambridge University Press, 1971.

Symons, James M. *Meyerhold's Theatre of the Grotesque: The Post-Revolutionary Productions, 1920–1932*. Coral Gables: University of Miami Press, 1971.

Valency, Maurice. *The Breaking String: The Plays of Anton Chekhov*. New York: Oxford University Press, 1966.

Yershov, Peter. *Comedy in the Soviet Theater*. Translated by Tanya Zuber. New York: Praeger, 1956.

Dissent

Blake, Patricia, and Hayward, Max, eds. *Dissonant Voices in Soviet Literature*. New York: Pantheon Books, 1962.

Bosely, Keith, comp. Introduction to *Russia's Underground Poets*, by Janis Sapiets. Selected and translated by Keith Bosley with Dimitry Pospielovsky and Janis Sapiets. New York: Praeger, 1969.

Browne, Michael, ed. Foreword to *Ferment in the Ukraine: Documents by V. Chornovil and Others*, by Max Hayward. New York: Praeger, 1971.

Brumberg, Abraham, ed. *In Quest of Justice: Protest and Dissent in the Soviet Union Today*. New York: Praeger, 1970.

Chornovil, Vyacheslav. Introduction to *The Chornovil Papers*, by Frederick C. Barghoorn. New York: McGraw-Hill, 1969.

Litvinov, Pavel. *The Demonstration in Pushkin Square: The Trial Records With Commentary and an Open Letter*. Translated by Manya Harari. Boston: Gambit, Inc., 1969.

Medvedev, Zhores A. *The Medvedev Papers: The Plight of Soviet Science Today*. New York: St. Martin's Press, 1971.

Reddaway, Peter, trans. and ed. *Uncensored Russia: Protest and Dissent in the Soviet Union: The Unofficial Moscow Journal "A Chronicle of Current Events."* New York: American Heritage Press, 1972.

Rothberg, Abraham. *The Heirs of Stalin: Dissidence and the Soviet Regime, 1953–1970*. Ithaca: Cornell University Press, 1972.

Scammel, Michael, ed. Foreword to *Russia's Other Writers: Selections from Samizdat Literature,* by Max Hayward. New York: Praeger, 1971.

Sjeklocha, Paul, and Mead, Igor. *Unofficial Art in the Soviet Union.* Berkeley: University of California Press, 1967.

Taubman, William. *The View from Lenin Hills: Soviet Youth in Ferment.* New York: Coward-McCann, 1967.

Van Het Reve, Karel. *Dear Comrade: Pavel Litvinov and the Voices of Soviet Citizens in Dissent.* Translated by Brian Pearce. New York: Pitman Publishing Corp., 1969.

Index

Specter of Alexander Wolf, The (Gazdanov), 33
Spinoza, Baruch, 1
Spisok blagodeyaniy (Olesha), 73
spravki, 162
Spusk pod vodu (Chukovskaya), 139
Sputniki (Panova), 57
Stalin, Joseph: First Five-Year Plan of, 25; succeeds Lenin in 1924, 29; speaks out for Soviet writers, 30; glorified, 45; Zamyatin's petition to, 47; régime, 60, 79; death of, 66, 68, 111, 139, 143; harnessed Russian nationalism to Communism, 67; attitude toward Bulgakov, 70–71; favored Bedny, 85; mentioned, 14, 18, 23, 32, 37, 40, 49, 51, 54, 71, 74, 82, 92, 94, 108, 110, 116, 132, 136, 140, 150, 152, 167
Stalinism, 119, 124, 129, 141, 145, 151
Stalin Prize, 55, 102, 103, 104, 105, 107, 108, 117, 123
Stanislavsky, Konstantin: producer of Chekhov's dramas, 1, 3, 4; death of, 79; theater, "the method" of, 80; mentioned, 7, 64, 66, 113
Stanislavsky School, 163
"Stantsiya Zima" (Yevtushenko), 120
Staraya sekretnaya (Gladkov), 53
State Literature Publishing House, 92
State Publishing House: publishes Yesenin's poetry, 22; mentioned, 149
State Realistic Theater of Red Presnya, 67
Steiner, Rudolf, 18
Stepanov, Alexander, 96
Stephanos (Bryusov), 87
Stevenson, Robert Louis, 1
Stikhi (Akhmatova), 92
Stikhi k Bloku (Tsvetayeva), 94
Stikhi o prekrasnoi dame (Blok), 19
Stikhi s dorogi (Prokofyev), 117

Stikhotvoreniya (Mandelshtam), 91
Stikhotvoreniya i poemy (Brodsky), 139
S toboi i bez tebya (Simonov), 107
Strakh (Afinogenov), 73
Strana Muraviya (Tvardovsky), 105
Stravinsky, Igor, 16, 18
Strindberg, August, 2
Strugatsky, Arkady, 118–19
Strugatsky, Boris, 118–19
Struna (Akhmadulina), 122
Studyonnoye more (Gherman), 55
Stukholov, Nikolai. *See* Pogodin, Nikolai
Sud idyot (Sinyavsky), 130
Sumasshedshiy korabl' (Forsh), 57
Surkov, Aleksei: description of Pasternak, 126; mentioned, 106
Surrealism, 46
Survey, a Journal of East & West Studies, 142
Suvorin, Aleksei, 3
Svad'ba (Simukov), 76
Svecha na vetru (Solzhenitsyn), 144
Svidaniye (Finn), 77
Svidetel' istorii (Osorgin), 33
Svyatoi kolodets (Katayev), 116
Symbolism, 64
Symbolists: Blok's allegiance to the, 19; mentioned, 10, 18, 83, 87, 88, 90, 93
Syn polka (Katayev), 97–98
Synu, kotorogo net (Inber), 57

Tairov, Alexander: productions of, 66–67
Tambov rebellion, 147
Tam gde byl shchastliv (Osorgin), 33
tamizdat: defined, 157–58; mentioned, 159, 160
Tarusskiye stranitsy, 140
Teatral'nyi roman (Bulgakov), 112, 113
Teffi, Nadezhda, 34

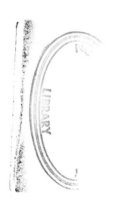